The Truth About What Nonprofit Boards Want

The Truth About What Nonprofit Boards Want

THE NINE LITTLE THINGS THAT MATTER MOST

June Bradham, CFRE
President, Corporate DevelopMint

John Wiley & Sons, Inc.

This book is printed on acid-free paper. ∞

Copyright © 2009 by June Bradham. All rights reserved.

Published by John Wiley & Sons, Inc., Hoboken, New Jersey.
Published simultaneously in Canada.

No part of this publication may be reproduced, stored in a retrieval system, or transmitted in any form or by any means, electronic, mechanical, photocopying, recording, scanning, or otherwise, except as permitted under Section 107 or 108 of the 1976 United States Copyright Act, without either the prior written permission of the Publisher, or authorization through payment of the appropriate per-copy fee to the Copyright Clearance Center, Inc., 222 Rosewood Drive, Danvers, MA 01923, 978-750-8400, fax 978-646-8600, or on the web at www.copyright.com. Requests to the Publisher for permission should be addressed to the Permissions Department, John Wiley & Sons, Inc., 111 River Street, Hoboken, NJ 07030, 201-748-6011, fax 201-748-6008, or online at http://www.wiley.com/go/permissions.

Limit of Liability/Disclaimer of Warranty: While the publisher and author have used their best efforts in preparing this book, they make no representations or warranties with respect to the accuracy or completeness of the contents of this book and specifically disclaim any implied warranties of merchantability or fitness for a particular purpose. No warranty may be created or extended by sales representatives or written sales materials. The advice and strategies contained herein may not be suitable for your situation. You should consult with a professional where appropriate. Neither the publisher nor author shall be liable for any loss of profit or any other commercial damages, including but not limited to special, incidental, consequential, or other damages.

For general information on our other products and services, or technical support, please contact our Customer Care Department within the United States at 800-762-2974, outside the United States at 317-572-3993 or fax 317-572-4002.

Wiley also publishes its books in a variety of electronic formats. Some content that appears in print may not be available in electronic books.

For more information about Wiley products, visit our Web site at http://www.wiley.com.

Library of Congress Cataloging-in-Publication Data:

Bradham, June.
The truth about what nonprofit boards want : the nine little things that matter most / June Bradham.
p. cm.
Includes index.
ISBN 978-0-470-45800-6 (cloth : acid-free paper)
1. Nonprofit organizations—Management. 2. Boards of directors. I. Title.
HD62.6.B73 2009
658.4'22—dc22
2009001891

Printed in the United States of America
10 9 8 7 6 5 4 3 2 1

Contents

Preface

The nonprofit arena is not what it used to be. But then again, neither is the rest of the business world.

Consider coffee. Years ago, Starbucks Coffee rid itself of traditional marketing. They abandoned mass advertising and set out to build endearing and enduring relationships with their customers, one cup at a time. Author John Moore shares how Starbucks' "sage advice and weathered truths exist solely in the hearts and minds of long-time Starbucks partners (employees)."

I love to hear, "One venti, nonfat, one Splenda, extra hot latte for June!" As I take my first sip, I think, wow, just the way I asked for it! But remember—it's not just the coffee, it's the experience. How do you feel when you walk into Starbucks? Do you look forward to paying a premium for delicious, flavorful, high-quality coffee? Do you mind waiting in line for the barista to know just how you want it? Do you think twice while you swipe a card for only a $4 purchase? Today, that answer is, "Absolutely I think about that purchase." Is it worth it?

The experience of serving on a nonprofit board should be no more complicated than a trip to Starbucks. Out of the mouths of those with good and bad experiences on nonprofit boards, this book exposes the real truth about what is at the core of a really good board experience, and what must be done to build solid, productive boards. Boards where the service is worth it. Great board members have spoken and they say it is the little things that count.

The nonprofit world is soaring through a period of change where we, too, must rid ourselves of our traditional approach to achieving our goals. Board leaders want staff members who form "enduring and endearing relationships" with their volunteers and donors. Therefore, just as Starbucks transformed the coffee break, we must begin transforming the nonprofit world—one board experience at a time.

When board members become members of our nonprofit *tribes* and join the ranks of those before them, they will learn through experience our own innate language. And when board members feel a sense of closeness with their chosen institution, one as close as the deepest friendship, we will know the tribe is formed. The nonprofit world will never be the same.

The Truth About What Nonprofit Boards Want shares candid comments from seasoned board members about their board experience—their tribal experience, if you will. Their thoughts dismiss myths many of us hold regarding nonprofit boards and teach all of us to communicate better with one another and our constituencies and magnify our impact as a direct result.

We are a trillion-dollar-a-year industry, adding more jobs than any other sector in the economy. We are serious partners with government and business. And the spotlight is on our work. Board work is more critical now than ever before. There are more and more universities, colleges, foundations, trade organizations, and consultants fighting over who gets to "educate and train" boards and staff. Nonprofits are getting entrepreneurial—creative financing, increased product development, partnerships with for-profits, and, in a really big way, circumventing face-to-face fundraising as people go looking for how to give on the Internet. Too bad few are listening to the truth: Ours is a Starbucks world.

That is why it is more competitive than ever to attract the best board members, train staff capable of creating the best board experience, and keep everyone around long enough to make a difference. Just like Starbucks, if the experience is good, if it is satisfying, the board will do its work. The number one indicator of success in the business world is profit. The number one worry of nonprofit leaders is funding to do the work and meet the mission. But giving or raising money is the *last* motivator for a seasoned board member to join a board. Their motivation is much simpler—it is the board experience. As a 30-year veteran in professional development work, this revelation brought me to my knees.

In this book, we will talk about the board experience—the unfettered truth. Not what staff does *to* the board. What staff does *with* them. Not what the board is to do for the organization. What we are to do *for* them. When the team has the right mix, the board will do their work and the money will follow.

At the conclusion of this book, I will do my best to tie it all together, giving you an idea of what a perfectly aligned organization looks like. One in which a staff leader can develop and implement a management plan in line with the emotional, social, and intellectual needs of a board member.

The drumbeat grows louder every day. In fact, in my many years of leading a for-profit company to help nonprofits be strategically and financially sound, I have never heard the drumbeat so loud. Why so loud? The challenge to meet nonprofit missions is enormous. Social need and charitable involvement is spreading throughout the world like a brush fire. As we race to solve social, educational, health, artistic, and environmental challenges, the people in control must be happy. If they believe deeply, and if we are charged up, I am confident we will be successful.

But where do we start?

The answer is simple: We must start with the experience, one that builds on the values of old leaders and infuses passion in the young ones. Much like John Moore, a long-time marketer, indicates for Starbucks to carry on the customer experience, the nonprofit staff members of tomorrow must infuse the board experience with work that is poignant, thought provoking, and actionable. We must all listen to the truth.

Good works abound throughout the world. In our quest to leverage social capital, there is one group of people worldwide who are critical to the success of any nonprofit: the board. Nonprofits want board members' reputations, talents, skills, and money. The board members know that. Volunteer leaders must begin to ask hard questions—not to settle for less from the organization they serve—to exceed their mission *and* to have a good personal experience. Board member by board member, a difference can be made. To make the difference, the key component must be wisdom—well-balanced wisdom called upon by all players.

This book is about the truth of the board experience. It's about what board members want. It's about the most satisfying board experiences as told by board members across three continents.

Of all the people interviewed, certain messages were consistent time and time again. No matter the type of board or the sophistication of the organization, the leaders I spoke to have a lot in common. On the pages that follow, you will find nine myths exposed, as well as the truths shared, all from the hearts and souls of the most giving, caring, and successful people I know. The points were much simpler than expected, but the whole of their message is much greater than the sum of its parts.

So grab a cup of coffee and get ready to learn a new language, one that will change your nonprofit experience forever . . .

—*June Bradham*

Introduction

Never before has the need for work without profit been so great. But the demands on time and resources have strained our survival in such a way that growth is altogether another story. Our response to this strain has been to focus on the structure and output of our organizations. But somehow, that just isn't working. The rules, regulations, and widely accepted thoughts about how we should act as professionals, what is expected of our board members, and what we should do *to* them are misguided and may be overshot. The impact on those on whom we depend is deep. It is the human element that we have been missing all along.

It is the little things that count the most. It is the big thinking, the wisdom of the board, that sets the pace. To make board thinking bold, the staff and board leadership must align. As leaders, staff members, and volunteers alike, the one thing we share is our humanity. We must relearn how to connect with one another, authentically communicate our thinking, and work together to achieve the mission.

Our focus must shift to engage not only the current generation of nonprofit board members but those who will follow in their footsteps. Their wants and needs, I believe, have been unclear to us thus far. This research has taught me that successful board experiences depend far more on the relationship among board members and with the chief staff person with whom they'll work, as well as with the personal meaning the nonprofit work has for each of them. The next generation is unlike any generation before them. And if we learn how to make the most of each person and their board experience, they will be our key to success.

Leaders across three continents opened their hearts to me and laid themselves bare by revealing their *wants,* which often are very disconnected from organizational needs. The organization *needs* things like policy, money, and legitimacy. The best board member *wants* things like a human connection and personal enrichment. The best board member wants to use his or her wisdom and skills to help the organization think and then act. The board member does not have *needs* that a nonprofit can fill, but the board member does have *wants.* The best CEO is able to uncover what each board member wants and give it to them. When this partnership flourishes, then the right board member will treat the organization right.

This book is here to reveal to you what board members *want.*

Throughout this book, we refer to the "CEO." This title can be used to mean the top officer of the organization or the top staff person with whom the board member works. In the case of higher-education institutions and hospitals with foundations, the CEO could have a double meaning: both the top administrative officer of the institution *and* the top executive officer of the foundation.

Study Design

To uncover the truth about *the board experience,* we started at the root: with board members.

I conducted months of face-to-face and telephone interviews over the course of a year, talking with highly involved board members from around the world. Combined, these leaders serve, or have recently served, on hundreds of boards, ranging from start-ups to the largest and most sophisticated organizations. Their missions represented all areas: university, health, arts, environment, religion, and human services. Regardless of type and background, size and specialty, all of these board members shared a similar message.

My findings have led me to present to you the nine most common myths about board work; these myths were dispelled in the candid statements from the board members who expressed some truths about what they really want. There is no doubt that the answers would not have been as uncensored had I not promised anonymity for those I interviewed as well as for their organizations. Each was someone I have worked with or met in social and educational circles. It was important that they trusted me enough to express their genuine and heartfelt stories.

The questions I asked were open-ended and focused on their experiences in nonprofit work. As you will see, their answers provided qualitative data that overwhelmingly revealed trends and expectations—wants—they have for a good board experience.

No great work is possible without a little help, and from some that help was enormous. There are several people who helped immensely with this book. The team from Wiley, who assisted from manuscript to publication. Kevin Mulvaney inspired me to get the project done and worked with me on critical thinking and writing. Jon McGann, PhD, with his uncanny ability to help me think through what is important, to uncover that information that was worth sharing with all of you. Meredith Short was at my side editing and managing the process at every step. Paula Harper Bethea, the most dedicated board leader I know, helped me understand the innuendo of board member experiences. And, of course, I cannot express enough thanks to my husband, Gil, who was my biggest cheerleader as I attempted this, my first book.

And to all the individuals who participated in these interviews, kudos to you, the wonderful board leaders who were so candid with their conversations and shared the most interesting stories! Among them were:

- Entrepreneurs who built and sold enough companies to have time to serve
- Executives with major companies ranging from Fortune 100 to Fortune 500
- An executive who founded a national consulting business and who was asked to build three separate major nonprofits with statewide influence and impact
- A retired executive who sold his information technology business and uses his spare time to serve on nonprofit boards in his new hometown
- A young mother, philanthropist, and civic leader who lives in three countries.
- A professional who has woven her career into civic service and is the first woman to chair the largest social service organization in the country
- A career volunteer and philanthropist who found her passion for service at her father's knee
- A former dean of nursing at a top-tier medical university who is now a philanthropist and ardent civic leader
- Philanthropists who have family offices to manage family affairs
- A few family fortune heirs and civic workers
- An entrepreneur who loves "turnaround opportunities" on the boards on which he serves
- The president of an international firm who is civically engaged but short on time

- A former consultant and officer of the largest consulting firm in the world
- And many more with similar backgrounds but with their own ideas about their best experiences

Spanning ages, geography, backgrounds, and interests, these wonderful board members readily shared their views.

Now enjoy their stories and our findings. Just listen to the truth.

It's the Cause, Not the Company.

THE TRUTH

Current board makeup is the number one reason a top-flight candidate will agree to consider board service—or will not.

Serving on a board is, after all, a voluntary activity. The experience has the opportunity to be satisfying and inspiring. At the very least it is a chance for members to work with a committed, intelligent team, one dedicated to making a difference. A board is not a country club; it is a band of dedicated brothers and sisters who have come together to make the world a better place. The key is that everyone at the table contributes and carries a share of the load.

What they say they want: connections to smart, accomplished, energetic people that they may already know or those they would like to know. Listen to the truth.

Board Story

I want a small group of board members I trust to get the job done.

> *"Much of the time I spend on board work is made worthwhile by the connections I make and what I pick up from fellow board members. We do well while doing good."*

As in life, there are those who are successful at every turn and others who, as my Dad used to say, are "late bloomers." That's what our leaders tell us. "The first thing I look at is who is listed on the left-hand side of the organization's stationery. If I like the list, I may listen to you about board service. If not, you don't have a prayer," said one board member who serves on four boards currently, ranging from a start-up to a well-run international organization.

He agreed with a fellow leader, who said, "I have served on boards for 20 years. I go much deeper than just the names. I ask a lot of questions about the work of the board. Are they really involved, or are they simply allowing their names to be used? I was appointed by the government to one public university, and to my dismay, after joining I have found that only a handful comprehend the basics of board work. Rather than thinking deeply, they just fret about things like admission numbers or marketing expense, not about what is driving numbers up or down."

This man shared with me the story of chairing an international arts nonprofit that was deeply in debt when he became chairman. In addition to the executive committee, he formed a management committee with two board members and the chair. "I wanted the ability to act when needed. The three of us focused on the mission and not ourselves. We disagreed, but we did it amicably." On this board there were 60 people. Many were there because they loved the cause. Others were there because of the impact the organization could make. Others were there, he said, "to fill out their resume."

In this case, the leader recruited a small band of brothers and sisters who drove fiscal policies, recruited a stronger board, launched and successfully completed a significant campaign, moved the organization into a beautiful and functional headquarters, and, most important, made a tremendous difference in the arts community. In seven years, he and his closest colleagues transformed an organization deeply in debt into one of the best-run arts organizations in the country.

"I wish I could just have nine people on a board who I know will think strategically, hammer it out, and at the end of the day just band together to get it done." He knows who he wants on his left and right side next time.

Board Story

I want to start with a blank slate. Then let me run with it.

> *"I gravitate to start-up situations where I have been given the freedom to set it all up—the board and the staff. When I can bring together complex characters, formulate a mutually shared vision, and enlist a highly participatory board of people who are very active and highly respected, I know we can elevate the sights of people to join our cause. Frankly, when you bring in money, you can drive policy."*

This elegant and dynamic woman prefers smaller boards, at least in the organizational phase. In establishing a public television foundation board years ago, she was given carte blanche to design the organizational structure as well as choose and recruit the board and staff. On another board, she gathered a highly committed group of respected leaders who traveled the state selling the idea of a School for Math and Science Foundation, as well as raising the funding for the buildings and programs for this public boarding school for exceptionally talented students. The governing board for the school was politically appointed.

As chair, she invited the governing board to meet jointly and frequently to build relationships and to further school policies the foundation board believed to be important. When I asked if there was resistance from the governing board, she said, "Of course not. They met with us because they wanted to know us."

As the foundation board brought in millions to fund the school, they were able to drive policy and bring the governing board to a new level. In this case, the self-selecting group provided what the politically appointed group wanted and needed: statewide awareness, credibility, and money. So while the politically appointed board did not have the stature that would attract her, the ability to shape the foundation board satisfied her and provided the lure to serve that is so very needed by board members. "As you look at board membership, if you don't think the board is enlightened, don't bother," she said. She knows how to make the right list of potential board members, check it twice, and then bring them on board. Nice.

Board Story

I want names on the letterhead I respect. And give me time to get to know them.

> *"I am sometimes shocked at the difference in what a board looks like on paper and how it acts in reality."*

This talented board member, new to his retirement city and home, jumped in and saved a local cultural organization with hard work. He brought in staff and board talent and moved things along with his gifts as well. He expressed disappointment in another recent board he joined. "The names looked great on paper, and I had heard great things about these folks. I must admit I was less interested in the mission of the organization than the people on the board. However, it seems to be little more than window dressing. The culture is to sit quietly and not ask questions. I am not sure this is the board for me. With this culture, there is no way for me to make a difference or get to know my fellow board members."

For this member, the board chair or executive director will need to recognize his bent for getting to an issue and helping solve it or he will fade away. At minimum, having social time before and after the meetings may help a member who wants to make new friends and will help the organization in return for meeting his need.

This board member goes on to say, "No board I am on is fully populated with an A-plus team. Many come only out of heart and don't bring skills or networks or money that are needed. Some are witnesses just filling a spot. Others are bright, articulate, dedicated, and skilled and can really get things done. I like to be with the latter."

Next time, I bet he will go well beyond "Who is on the board?" to "Who are they?" and "what are they doing?"

Board Story

I want to know a wide variety of smart, accomplished people.

"One of my favorite boards has 50 members . . . a university board composed of government appointees, faculty, staff, students, and alumni. I have come to know people I never would have known this well otherwise. When we make

decisions, every constituency is at the table. This makeup has a huge potential for disaster, but we work together for the good of the university."

This woman, like many with whom we work is passionate about her service. She has been chairman of almost every organization on whose board she has served. In her university, the board was composed of governmental appointees, presidential appointees, faculty, staff, students, and alumni. I immediately asked her if I had misunderstood.

I had not.

We agreed that this had a huge potential for disaster. However, in reality, it has had a great deal of success. Why? All of the constituent groups were represented. No one could sweep anything under the rug and make decisions for others! Imagine that!

This active woman speaks to two primary reasons this has worked: "The president of the university is beloved and trusted. He is fair and open at all times. And he makes sure that before and after every meeting there is scheduled informal time for all of us to get to know each other. There are many occasions where we are thrown together socially: retreats, university occasions, committee meetings, and much more. We have more respect for each other because we know each other. We know about each other's children, illnesses, accolades, businesses, trips, and more. We are not a nameless group. We are real people with mutual respect, intellect, and trust. We work together for the greater good of the university, so it works."

So, even a very large group can be highly attractive to this high value board member when she's given the opportunity to know them.

Board Story
I want to use my brain.

> *"I am at the point that I want to be on a small board, no more than 12 people. I want my fellow board members to have best-in-class skill sets. We can scrub an issue and get something done."*

This young man chairs the board of a Fortune 500 company. That experience is the gold standard, as it is for many of the board members I interviewed for this book. "The for-profit company board 'rings all the bells' for me," he says. "All of the board members are outside directors with world-class skill sets. I love that board because what we do is fun, we are engaged in stuff we should be, and we get things done."

No nonprofit experience can come close to this for-profit for him. However, he has a love for the environment and is willing to work to save the planet. He can be on any board he wants. But what he wants is to serve on small organizations with big, meaningful goals. "People like me love chewing on an issue in an intellectual debate about what we do next. When expected to be a rubber stamp type, you have not dipped into my brain."

Considering his experience, he refuses to be on any board that has no fiduciary responsibility. An automatic "no" comes with any request to serve on any advisory boards or boards of visitors because "all they want is my money. They want to spoon-feed me at a meeting and next week send a gift officer over to look at my paintings. I hate that. Use me intellectually or I tire of it quickly."

June's Thoughts

Seasoned board members prefer a small group of people they can count on to do the serious work of the board. Unless starting a new initiative, leaders look for current board strength to warrant acceptance. While a great cause is important, it's not typically enough for someone to choose to serve on a board. The names are important, of course, but the good news is that this isn't totally self-serving. Having highly respected members on your board will give you a first pass for a positive discussion about an invitation to join the board.

To raise money and increase visibility you must look for board members with both the respect and profile to attract others, as well as the ability and willingness to use their connections. That is what you need. But what do they want? They want to be with people they know they can trust already or someone they want to get to know. Board members will serve your cause if you are serving theirs. Some want to choose the small group that will move the cause forward, while others find new friends they can highly respect and will be even more motivated to work for the cause.

What is the board member's reward? It is either a new network or, at the very least, a deeper one. Many times, fellow board members become close friends, and even more often, their relationships serve as a way for their business to flourish.

What do you get? Their reputation, connections, work, and projects accomplished for your cause. If the experience is good enough, and their passion for the mission deepens over time, you get their significant financial support as well.

Historically, these highly sought after individuals have come from a small band of brothers and sisters—a flock, a tribe. Today, there is more wealth and influence among people who do not belong to such a tribe of elites. These entrepreneurial leaders are busy and may well be unknown. Opportunities abound for nonprofit executives to find the next wave of board members as a way of connecting with a board member whose name is already on the list. The challenge is to bring the high potential but unseasoned board members into the fold of the board as quickly as possible—and be sure they are welcomed, challenged, and get what they want. So you can get what *you* want.

Among the articulate, successful, driven decision makers you pursue, consider not only the talents and interests of those you recruit, but also put some thought into who they know and who they might wish to know.

The first thing a prospective board member does is look at the names on the left side of the letterhead. Every time. Every interview. Everybody said this. First! These leaders say serving on a board is an honor and a deep responsibility. The seasoned people you want on your board will think first about who would be their partners at the board table. These folks like success. They believe it starts with the leaders and spreads throughout the winning team. Building a board is not unlike planning the most interesting dinner party.

Often, the first step to success is based on the question, "Who is coming to dinner?"

I have searched the literature thoroughly for data that talks about the meaning of the need for ultimate respect among fellow board members—a big part of what creates the board experience. There is nothing new on this topic as my board leaders describe it. All literature points toward a grid to have a broad range of people, looking at talents or geography or diversity. That's all right with my group if—but only if—the qualification for board nomination is not diversity for diversity's sake. Players with the capacity to lead, a willingness to make a real difference, and the network to help the organization move forward in some meaningful way all matter greatly. They just do.

A Great Board Member Is a Great Board Member. Period.

THE TRUTH

The board member who doesn't feel the cause passionately from head to toe can't compete with one who does.

All of us change over time. Early in life, most of us are flattered when someone we respect invites us to a board seat. *Who* asks us to join is enough to make us want to engage. At that point, just learning to be on boards and meeting new people is challenging, just as learning any sport is challenging in the beginning. Just as the bunny slope is not challenging once you have conquered skiing a Black Diamond slope, highly experienced board members change, too, they tell us, with time.

We now know absolutely that these board members want smart, articulate volunteer partners. But there is more. It must be the right group coupled with a cause that stirs passion. Without passion, even the most accomplished board member will not engage. In fact, the more seasoned a board member, the more passion is required.

Hear them talk about a subtle but oh-so-important change. Listen to the truth.

Board Story

Member to buddies—Ask away but if I don't really want to do this, I will be the empty seat.

> *"I just need to have the gumption to say no if I am not committed, no matter who asks. When I do not do that, I hate going to the meetings and I am a horrible board member."*

Recently, this man's bank chairman asked him to serve as chairman of the city's largest social services campaign. This board member has served as chairman of that organization in every city in which he has lived over the past 30 years. While he admires the organization greatly and is a member of their top giving society, he will accept the job this time because of who asked, but he knows his passion runs low. "Been there, done that," he said.

He has three boards that he loves: the arts board because of the learning and the high-level fundraising; the small university because it is his wife's school and he admires the president; and a medical university foundation board because it is a research and teaching institution making a real scientific and clinical difference for human beings in the world. For all three, his financial acumen and creative financing are critical to optimizing every penny. Each organization is vastly different. Each needs him in a different way. Each has some good board members and an excellent chief executive officer (CEO). The arts organization has the highest-level board members and provides the most fun. The small university has a CEO he respects, and they really need his guidance. The medical university has a strong mission and a triple-A president. He is engaged. He is passionate. And the chairman's board? He feels stuck.

Board Story

I have the gumption, but do I have the passion?

> *"There is a direct correlation between my passion and my favorite organizations. The best experience is with those boards I chose. My company is very generous. We have our pick of the boards we want. My two favorite current boards are an arts organization because it is fun, has great people, and is a place I can learn. The second is an up-and-coming small university with a visionary president. On both, I have the influence to direct significant gifts, and I do."*

On the arts board, he is a businessperson who wants to learn more about the arts. He loves the meetings where he is taught why a performance is considered excellent. He loves learning the names of performers considered the best in the world at what they do and the cheerful environment of the arts festivals and parties—great people in a great environment. All things are congruent, and he likes the mission a lot. This man can have his pick of boards! I was amazed to hear him talk of his personal attraction to a few nonprofits. He admires and is flattered to be with board members he respects in these organizations and is passionate about what they do. His company makes a significant contribution because it is good for the organizations and good for the company. He and his wife make significant contributions in addition because they love the work of the organization and because he knows he must be a personal player to maintain his leadership position. For that reason, he never minds "writing that check" to organizations that stir his deep and genuine interest.

He represents his company on his choice of boards—ones where he has personal passion.

Board Story
I want to leave before I get bored.

> *"Who asks me is very important. I won't even entertain board service unless the board is right for me and I am personally asked by a current board member whom I really respect. However, I will now turn down that person if I cannot find a personal passion for the work of the organization or look forward to interacting with the CEO and my fellow board members. Passion comes when the organization is adept at combining the work of the board with fun, an organization on the path to real change and a place where talents are used and valued. But before I lose that zest, before I get bored, I need to move on."*

This individual loves board service and spends most of her days working for organizations. But one organization, as a personal passion, stands out among them all. She has spent 28 consecutive years on a social services board at all levels: local, state, national, and international. This organization, for her, is the most effective in connecting those who need and those who serve their needs. At every step of the way, she has felt immediate gratification when she has made someone's life better, and she believes this organization is unique in that. Even when she was the national chair, she was in a local nonprofit on every trip, so she continued to see the good work that was being done. After 28 years, though, it was time for her to back away. Not because she was no longer interested, but "because no board member should stay beyond their time." She would not go back on one of their boards, not because she doesn't care about their work, but rather because she has done all that she can do. Her creativity drives her passion and she is out of new ideas. Lucky is the next organization that captures her interest!

Board Story

I have the passion. Without the respect of my fellow board members, it is not enough.

> *"My least favorite board quite simply wasted my goodwill. The board meetings were endless and all about scrambling for money rather than focusing on mission. Every meeting was chaos, starting with an agenda and ending with chatter that led to no strategy."*

This organization serves unwed mothers. It was going through a culture change. The past generations "hid" the unmarried pregnant girls at this home until birth, when the girls often gave their babies up for adoption. Today, the organization houses young women who have no place to go or are in a threatening environment. Additionally, they do many outreach and educational programs surrounding teen pregnancy. This organization had attracted a few highly skilled and valued board members who organized a fabulous garden festival that raised hundreds of thousands of dollars each year and gave the home visibility.

Eventually, though, a coup occurred between the old-guard and the new-guard leadership. The old guard voted against doing the garden festival in the future! High-value board members resigned from the board, and this board member came in as a "healer." She made very generous annual gifts and bought special things the home needed. A trained nurse in her past life, she had passion for the cause. She also started a new and very profitable event that became popular with mothers, grandmothers, and children. If you can believe this, the old guard voted down the continuation of yet another very lucrative event for the organization! Needless to say, this board member resigned, feeling "they wasted my goodwill."

Today, the organization is threatened with closure. This board member has moved on to organizations that value her passion, skills, wisdom, and generosity.

Board Story

I want to help passionate leaders I admire.

> *"Of course who asks you is critical. But my trusted neighbor must be accompanied by the president. I actually really love helping someone I admire accomplish something they are passionate about. Their passion somehow rubs off on me."*

This board member has gotten choosy over time. It is definitely not just what he can do for the organization but how the organization can satisfy his need to make a real difference. The top executive officer must build a connection between the board and the organization. The best have been where the executive made him feel like she was working for him. Where he feels the most passion, however, is a local university 20 minutes from his home.

The university funnels people into the local economy: nurses, police, teachers, MBAs, and more. These are people needed to keep his very wealthy community running. The people on the board are the highest level of civic-minded philanthropists and business leaders. They have a great cause they can all get excited about, and they are led by a great president. "This is fun," he said, "and when I lived in the major business city in the United States, because I did not have enough generations of ancestors on a board, I would have never been able to make a real difference." Here, he is appreciated, he is excited, and he looks forward to making it all happen. He stressed that his passion is more deeply stirred by wanting to help a respected staff person achieve something good than he is moved by the mission. A different passion, but one that is valid to him nonetheless.

Board Story

I want to be where I want to be.

> *"Early in my career, I was flattered, honored really, that the top leader in the community would take the time to call on me personally to ask me to serve on a board. So I enthusiastically said yes. No more. Now I only want to be, well, where I want to be."*

There are two boards this individual has very much enjoyed. For him, the easiest thing is to write a check, but he does not find that satisfying. Writing a check has not done much for his self-esteem, nor has it made him feel very worthy. Most of the organizations he deals with need money. He needs something else entirely.

This philanthropist said that it is meaningful to him for someone to make some real effort to recruit him to the board: the executive who takes a day of his time traveling for a personal visit to talk about an organization he cares about. "If a busy volunteer goes out of his way to tell me about why he is so enthusiastic about the cause, I will look more deeply. But I must say I am getting a little more cynical and more difficult to recruit. If the main appeal to me is 'come help me fix it,' then I am probably going to jump in. You see, I am not afraid of losing business because I have some skin in the game to change an executive or push for some hard choices. I am a turnaround guy for an organization that wants that."

As we talked more about passion, he said, "Over the past 20 years I have a good record of fixing messed-up institutions. I am not afraid to have failure in my life. One of the most passionate things I did was chair a philharmonic orchestra through bankruptcy. That grew passion, let me tell you."

His passion is making a real impact more than simply supporting the cause. The next organization to get him better be ready for change to keep him engaged.

Board Story

I want to bring transformational change. Give me the project. Let me feel the passion.

> *"It is still very important to me to have confidence in the person who asks me to serve and I feel I must honor our relationship by doing a good job: fundraising or governing. I have learned, however, if I do not personally get excited about the cause, I will work at 40 percent capacity."*

"I can remember my first encounter when asked to serve on the community-wide campaign for human services funding by the chairman of the biggest company in my community. I was awed that he would choose me. I worked my heart out and, consequently, have been asked to serve on numerous boards over the past 30 years. Recently, my friend, the president of my university, asked me to chair the biggest campaign in the history of the university. It is time for me to give back to the place I got my start but also to help a person I admire. I am passionate about the challenge. I probably should have thought it through a little more because I have been away from the state and the university for so long, but here I am and I am enjoying making progress."

He describes the progress this way: Before accepting the chair position, he wanted to be sure the campaign would be truly transformational. The president allowed a few of his fellow board members to form a committee composed of "gold standard" people who would challenge each other and the university with great thinking. They started with understanding the resources available in the university to achieve greatness. They involved professors and smart volunteers. They ended up understanding what it would take to transform the university and they got the commitment for staff and infrastructure to make it happen. Now they have the house in order and are raising almost a billion dollars. "That much will transform. Anything less will not. Is that satisfying? You bet."

But he was quick to point out that he did not do this work wholly because of who asked him. He did it to transform the organization. But if the president had not asked, he would not have agreed. This reinforces the notion that both passion *and* who asks someone to get involved are the clear winners for why a board member jumps at the chance to participate.

June's Thoughts

As board members grow in experience, who asks them to participate diminishes in importance. Don't get me wrong, who asks is still critical, but a seasoned volunteer will turn down even the most influential contact if they cannot "feel the passion." Too often, they will agree to the request from someone to whom they "just cannot say no." What happens next, they say, is that they become the empty seat on the board. They just cannot muster the enthusiasm to get engaged. Their involvement will be minimal at best.

The issue of a "right fit" is critical. Not just the right fit for the organization, but the right fit for the volunteer. Just because a board member is a superstar on the board of the Red Cross doesn't mean he'll be just as stellar on the symphony's board. Before asking someone to serve, make sure you know them.

If they don't seem to have that burning desire to serve your organization, don't invite them to join just because they're good guys or have served other boards well or are the moneybags of the region.

Too often, we get caught up in the value of a name. But the dedication and drive of a committed and appropriate board member can far outweigh the value of someone who comes from the right family or the right company. It is critical to not only define the role of the board member in your organization but how the organization will handle the board member. Make the experience a great one for both of you. As you court a new leader, it is imperative to be completely honest about expectations. You must be willing to ask questions to get to the root of their passion. And you must have the courage to recognize if "the fit" isn't there.

Presidents and CEOs often face search committees, development officers are put to the test with multiple board interviews, and administrative assistants have their backgrounds checked. In much the same way, great attention to detail is imperative when seeking new board members. They can have a profound impact, positively or negatively, on the culture of your board and thus on the rise or fall of your organization. If they aren't excited, let them off the hook.

It is interesting that passion in these board members was not always for the cause, the mission. More often than not, it was passion for the leadership or the real work the board member could do to transform an organization.

Sure, you need them. But you probably don't if they really don't want you. If it's not a good match, move on.

The Board Alone Is Responsible for Success or Failure.

THE TRUTH

Without a dedicated, smart, visible, and vocal CEO at the helm, a board will not totally engage.

A successful relationship between the CEO and the board is challenging. CEOs must have the right personality and skill set to fit with the organization and its board. Their vision, however, must be shared without force-feeding the board. They must be a white knight but with little ego. Stories about the CEO relationship were told with more passion than any other subject. Why is it that some have the ultimate professional relationships and others do not? Listen to the truth.

Board Story

Board to CEO—I want to help. But if you don't really need it, don't ask me.

"The board on which I am most active is definitely not the most elite board. Nonetheless, we only want the best CEO.

The mismatch in this relationship requires my top-tier CEO to rely more on the board because she does not have the staff in place to address the most challenging work. That is a tough call for a leader who may have to spend a lot of time nurturing a board when she would prefer to just tell someone to get the job done."

A bright, young entrepreneur is serving on his mother's college board. The best anywhere around in structural restoration, he is asked to chair the facilities committee. "Perfect fit for me," he says. "I decided to throw myself into this. I put teams together to search and survey the entire campus, develop comprehensive plans. I worked with the board to find an innovative way to fund the critical needs. Our president had no one on staff to undertake such a study. I spent months on this and was excited by what I could bring to the college. What happened? No vote. Nada. Nothing. And, even more insulting, the next year I was not even on the facilities committee! The new committee head has not even called a meeting this year, to my knowledge." He goes on, "I have been examining my life. I am young and successful financially. I feel wonderful about my career. I think the next decade may be focused on service to humanity in giving and working with nonprofits."

In this situation, this leader admires the work of the president and respects her a great deal. The problem here is that the board member was asked to take on a task but his work was not really wanted. It ended up being busy work as he saw it.

Do you think this leader will spend his time or intellectual capital again on behalf of this college? Will they be the recipient of his greatest generosity? We shall see.

Board Story

Board to CEO—If you need me, use me. Then you have me.

> *"I was on the board of a major medical university foundation. The only role of this board is to manage funds. The president of the foundation and his team are highly capable of managing the money and hiring money managers. However, the staff engaged the board in the exciting and highly involved process of setting policy for asset allocation, choosing the money managers and more. We had a team of five of the brightest and most successful board members charged with this project. We were on conference calls from our vacation homes, we cut short trips to make meetings, I had to really stretch to learn and research information to become knowledgeable enough to stand tall with my peers. I got to know my fellow board members in a way that would never have happened just attending meetings. I know I made a real difference and am more committed to the organization than ever."*

This talented woman is a board member who takes any role assigned very seriously. In this case, she was asked to chair the task force to oversee the policies and talent to manage a very large endowment. Without deep financial experience, she had to learn and stretch to be a good financial leader. Other members of the team were experienced in significant financial management careers. What made the CEO good here? He asked for and allowed the board to lead the work of setting policy and financial management. The CEO of this organization is a former high-level banker and greatly skilled. He had the grace, smarts, and courage to step aside and let the leaders lead. Board members get truly involved when they are welcomed into the organization, believe in its management, and are challenged by the tasks. Thanks to a positive experience, one that is poignant, thought provoking, and actionable, this board member is wed to the organization and looks forward to what the CEO puts out for her next.

Board Story

Board to CEO—When we know what we are doing, we are going to dabble in your pie.

> *"The CEO needs to develop a strategy to gain board approval and be willing to defend it to the death. The board needs to dip into their brains and challenge the CEO to continue to raise the standards."*

This curious and energetic board member wants the staff to "thoroughly scrub the strategic direction for the organization and be prepared to challenge the board if necessary to defend that direction in an open, even argumentative debate." He works with one environmental organization that has a top-tier founding executive director and a mission in which he believes. The executive's passion, of course, is the work on the environment. Historically, however, the board thought the financial oversight and controls were weak. As the board became populated with more board members with "best-in-class" financial skill sets, the scrutiny of the financials became a focus. Two of the most talented board members with financial acumen told the executive that they were uncomfortable and wanted to raise the standards in this arena. They worked for months developing fiduciary policies, examining the records, searching for a chief financial officer (CFO). Then they worked with the CFO over a period of time to be sure she understood the board's expectations and was doing the work to meet their standards. Now the finance report is refined, a good comptroller is in place, and the reporting has improved fourfold. "We fixed what was broken."

When I asked how the executive director reacted to the forward movement on the board's part, he said, "It was a slight struggle, not because the executive thought what we wanted to do was not the right thing to do. The executive director thought the time and attention to finances would take him away from focusing on the mission each week." His fellow board members made a real difference. They used their intellect and skills to correct financial issues for the long haul.

"If you are going to have strong-minded people on the board, the executive director must let them dabble in things." If the leader is too territorial, this high-quality board member just will not stay.

Board Story

Board to CEO—I want you to be sincere. Please do not manipulate me.

> *"Good management is synonymous with serious and meaningful governance. At my two favorite boards, the level of intelligence and care was so high I only needed to say something once. The team understood what I said and worked on it. They had tremendous respect for my time, skills, intellect, and integrity. First and foremost, they allowed a relationship to form between governors and staff that was full of respect and trust. Never did I feel anything was hidden. It was a partnership."*

This powerhouse shared the story of a VP for advancement who knew how to befriend people in a way that is not sneaky or opportunistic. He recognizes what leaders want and motivates them to do that. At the same time, he runs a tight ship. If a young person joined his team and he saw in them the talent, motivation, culture, and education to be great, he pulled out all the stops to teach them. They shadowed him, had conferences with him. He pushed, helped, taught. They learned and grew. But if one was hired who did not have the potential, he got rid of them immediately. He treated the staff with the utmost respect. His stewardship program was unparalleled. He had understanding and creativity. He worked with the president to focus fundraising on academics. He brought the faculty onto his side immediately with this focus, so they brought in all their contacts and worked hard to help the university succeed. "Every conversation we had was sincere and clear. If I was asked to take a task, it was meaningful and needed. My work was appreciated and respected."

This was an unusually happy university board member. Many of our board champions complained that universities are often too "buttoned up" to need much meaningful help from board members. Not this one. The difference? The CEO knew how to engage the board even when he could have done the work himself.

Board Story

Board to CEO—We want you to be successful. That means get the right board and pay you well.

"A consultant did a retreat for my college. He said most not-for-profits are poorly run because we cannot afford to handle great talent. So the college limps along, unlike the corporate world where we could put the resources in and get the output."

You just have to love this guy. He is wealthy by his own admission, entrepreneurial, and deeply passionate about good works in the world. He is and has served on search committees and struggles with all of them. The words of the consultant have come back to him so many times: "Can we not afford to handle great talent?" Board members are fiduciary agents, of course. Often, this board member says, the board "wants the best person for the lowest cost." That translates often to the thought that spending adequately to hire the best talent to move the organization forward just doesn't feel right to nonprofit board members, who, he says, "are all too focused on the numbers rather than the mission." He enjoys board work and thrives on it when the right CEO is in place. "Many organizations are simply too thrifty and end up with a second or third choice of leaders." These words—"can we not afford to hire the best talent?"—haunted him so much that he bought copies of *Forces for Good* for all of his fellow board members and asked them to read it before the next meeting of the search committee. This book outlines new organizations that are considered great. One common denominator? A great CEO.

"I continue to strive to solve this problem: How can we as boards not afford to hire the best talent?" he asks.

I wonder how many CEOs will read this and call to get his name. I promised anonymity, remember?

Board Story

Board to CEO—We want you to have the vision, do the homework, and ask the board to make the decision or close the deal.

"For me, the CEO is critical. I often find myself on search committees looking for the right person. I think the CEO must be more of an articulate leader, even more than a manager, if

the organization can absorb that. CEOs have to handle big-time entrepreneurs with huge egos on their boards. We can talk big and give big money, but they have to be able to articulate their vision in a way we find exciting and credible."

Entrepreneur, hard thinker, soft heart. This board member has little patience for long stories, data, or slides. Just tell him the facts. But if you don't touch his heart, you won't get his leadership or his money. His most satisfying experience is a camp for sick kids who pay no fee but have a week of being like all kids. He is proud of the new executive director who is managing the board, setting the vision, directing the board to big decisions about expansion and endowment. He says, "Over the past 20 years I have a good record of fixing really messed-up institutions. I like to get the plan and then find the paid leader who can work the plan. They better be able to handle my pace and ego. If they can, they've got me for life." He says, "I am not afraid of failure. I don't want the CEO to worry about that either. If they are too skittish, they won't do anything bold. If it isn't bold, they will never make a difference." He is looking for the deep impact that a brave, determined, articulate CEO can make.

Board Story

Board to development staff—Guide us. But the development officer is not the president.

"The VP of advancement is not the president. The director of development is not the executive director. I work with talented and articulate advancement and development people. When I am going on a seven figure and above call, as nice as they are, they cannot close the deal. If the institution's CEO doesn't feel this is a priority enough to go with me, that is the last call I will make."

This leader is wealthy and runs with others who are. He prefers for-profit boards because they are "no nonsense." On corporate boards, the goal is simple: shareholder value. He feels like it gets all soft on nonprofit ones. He likes a CEO or president who knows what he wants and tells him what that is and what he wants the board to do. Then he wants the development folks to have all the information about the folks they are going to call on. If they line up dates for him and the president, he will get the appointment. The president will tell the story. He will share the board member's passion. Then, together, they will make "the ask." It drives this board member crazy when the "development folks can't swallow their egos enough to not go. This is the deal of the peer and the president. Period."

He told me the story of the turnover of a great president and the development staff. In this case, the development staff was perfect for their jobs, except, he says, those who wanted to be the public face of the institution. "When the development officer wants to be the president, it just doesn't work. The president needs to be front and center."

The development staff and the CEO need to know who the board member is more comfortable with in approaching their peers.

June's Thoughts

Those who lead nonprofits defy labels. But the road before them is not always easy. Staff turnover in nonprofits continues at a rapid pace. Leadership is often misaligned. And the most desired board members are stretched thin. How can we fix this?

One solution is AlignMint™. If we are to make a transformation, we must ensure staff and board experiences are positive. Board and staff must not only be clear about their organization's mission but be in agreement about how to accomplish that work.

An aligned organization must have an executive with skills and personality appropriate to manage and support a fantastic board experience. This often requires individualized, appropriate engagement of each board member. Equally important is a board with wisdom and assets to lead the organization and deep engagement in the endeavor. When AlignMintgt™ happens, we will less often witness a deadwood board or staff leaders frustrated daily about lack of funding or board understanding.

I have served both as an executive director and as the chairman of nonprofit boards and I am the founder and president of a for-profit company dealing with nonprofits and their leaders. I have experienced firsthand, from every angle, that every organization or institution must attract the level of executive and board appropriate to their needs at the time. As the organization evolves in its knowledge and ability to deliver a service to its constituents, so must the board and staff evolve in their ability to lead the organization.

The innate challenge is that the organization can change its strategy and begin new work immediately. The organization can determine that the executive is no longer the right fit and can be invited to depart. The board, however, takes years to reshape. Often, it can take between 6 and 12 years to replace board members as they come up for reelection. If time is of value to you, which I suspect it is, and you want to do it in two years or less, alignment of your board and your CEO is important. We use The AlignMint™ model—one that has been implemented by Corporate DevelopMint for the past 20 years in various incarnations and now has been pulled together into one cohesive plan to transform organizations from mediocre to excellent. From dysfunctional to highly functional.

Successful alignment must begin with the chief executive wanting things to change, for the vision, board, and staff to be appropriate to achieve optimum success. Sometimes it can start with the executive's leaving and the board's demanding change.

There must be alignment among the board, the organization, and the CEO. When that alignment is out of order, there is dissatisfaction among all players. AlignMint™ helps boards and executives better fit the players with the scope of the mission and level of function of the nonprofit. A thorough and insightful understanding of the current situation of the organization and its inner workings juxtaposed with the demands from the organization's constituencies must be fully synthesized into a strategic plan. This plan must carefully and honestly articulate the strengths and challenges of the alignment of the organization, board, and staff. At this point, brave and highly capable leadership can make the changes necessary to realign the organization. As organizations go through the AlignMint™ process with a seasoned current or interim executive in place, only the best future for the organization and those it serves is in focus. All parties can speak freely and, in the end, the organization is forever changed.

Yes, the best leaders of nonprofits defy labels. Board members expect the CEO to be "buttoned up." Often, a highly competent CEO does not want to endure board members "dabbling in her pie." That is a problem for the board experience. As you read their quotes and stories, our board leaders support that theory. Sure, a great CEO can run the organization. If that CEO wants the board's network, reputation, and money, she better be good at letting them get into something meaty. Board leaders want a CEO who is driven to achieve broad social change, whatever the organization. But they also want to feel they have been the designers of the change. Sound a bit like Starbucks? The company was started with an "unrelenting passion for rewarding everyday moments." Similarly, we are responsible for meeting our board members' wants, not their needs. It is the little things that CEOs do that really count.

CEO and Board Members Are Colleagues. Nothing More.

THE TRUTH

Engaged boards have an inspired CEO who forms a partnership with board members and demonstrates a passion for the mission while keeping ego in check.

These leaders believe that the chef should be five-star even if the guests are three-star. Board members should search for and attract to the organization the most talented top executive possible, regardless of comparable board sophistication. The smart, thoughtful, passionate CEO will attract and retain the best and most appropriate board members regardless of whether the organization is Oxford or the local food bank. Board members want to engage with a leader who inspires and stimulates but does not lead with an iron fist. Listen to the truth.

Board Story

The best chief needs me to make real transformational change. That's what I want, too.

"I gravitate to people, not projects. If I believe in the leader, find them compelling and visionary, if I believe they can pull

the project off, if they want my help, not just my money, then I am more likely to truly engage."

This board member believes that there is "no way for nonprofits to be as stimulating as for-profits, mostly because of the amount of pressure that is brought to bear by those who are always focused on the need for money, yet offer little true social change in return." He sees many nonprofits led by less-than-inspiring directors wanting to do what they want but not necessarily what you want. "They are always looking to boards to be quiet and go get the money."

However, he described one excellent experience this way: A college president wanted to transform a local college. He came to the board and told them what he needed to get the job done and told them how much money he needed to accomplish the task. Then he told them to "go get it done and we said, 'Yes, sir!'"

Why? The president had a vision that would transform the region where the board member lives. And this was a top-tier president for this school who had to wear so many hats that the one thing the board could really do was bring in their contacts. The president could close the deal, the advancement folks could organize it, and the board member in short order got the folks with the cash to come to the table. In this case, the president did not mince any words about what he needed. The board member could introduce a few valued relationships. The president was inspirational and passionate about the mission. He got what he needed.

So did the board member.

Board Story

Board to CEO—I want to be inspired, not ruled.

"I want a strong and passionate CEO, but she needs to know that she is there to execute the policy and strategic direction

> *of the board. Sometimes CEOs are so headstrong they try to 'overlead.'"*

This individual was on the board of a hospital that was sold to a for-profit health company. A conversion foundation resulted. Before he was named chair of the new foundation, the hospital board made the decision to hire a director and two assistant directors. "Frankly," he said, "this was a foundation model sold to the hospital board that was the vision of the new executive director." Bylaws were written and the wrong staff and board horses engaged; the leadership and the organization were not aligned. "The board was weak and the staff was strong," he said. "On the board there were three strong members who did not believe the direction of the foundation was right for the community." This chairman worked delicately to remove the director, reduce the staff, and eventually change the board composition. "Now, there is alignment among the board, the staff and the organization" that he believes is right for the community.

Beware of the powerful board member who feels the staff manipulates the board. The board will win most of the time.

Board Story

Board to CEO—I want you to be a visionary and strong leader. It is a delicate balance.

> *"Sometimes a CEO can become too headstrong. If he wants something to happen too much and the board is divided, making it happen at all costs is just the thing to cost him his job."*

This leader is so strong that he is sought after internationally. He wants a staff that is strong and visionary. He has watched with interest, however, deeply ingrained staff believe they have the last word and become so determined to make something happen it becomes for them a career-ending decision (CED). In the case he described to me, a powerful grant-making foundation leader became so determined to construct a building that he divided the board. That division resulted in his "early retirement." Had this good, long-term staffer engaged the board in meaningful dialogue and let them determine the outcome, he would still be there.

Board Story

The president must force politically appointed boards to be visionary.

> *"Politically appointed boards are set up for mediocrity. Unless the president is strong and forces the board to deal with visionary issues, the meetings are just full of nothing interesting. The best board meetings are those in which the members understand the meaning of duty, loyalty, and care. Do they dig into the budget, asking questions and seeking to understand?"*

This fine man was appointed by the governor to a university board of trustees. He gives most of his fellow board members a grade of C. Few have run companies or been on significant boards. He feels he has nothing to lose, so he uses his perspective from big corporate boards to influence the running of this billion-dollar enterprise. "I push some things that make a difference. I know something about what's going on because I dig deep into budgets and plans. I spend a lot of time studying the workings of the institution. I do not get into management issues, but I do set the bar high for management. The board meetings are interesting because we learn about high-level research and treatment of difficult diseases. The work of the university is exciting, so I am charged up to make it a place that as much positive can happen as possible. The board meetings? Not fun. They are merely learning experiences. Serving on the executive committee and interfacing with the very smart and aggressive president? Fantastic! It is just so hard to move the needle in a political bureaucracy."

Board Story
I want the chief to watch her ego.

> *"I was attracted to an international board of an organization that builds employment for villages in the Middle East. I like it because it benefits so many women who need the help. But the CEO running it is a self-promoter and that is distasteful to me. On another organization, a carpenter with a few dollars and a big heart inspires me."*

This international leader serves on boards all over the world, including one that is building a university solely focused on philanthropic studies in the Middle East. The staff of one mideastern charity is "hiding behind the guise of helping women, and I think it is cowardly. They want my name and my money but they don't want my leadership." She talks of this staff as building a dysfunctional and fragmented board. Travel to these board meetings is difficult and time consuming, and the only value of the board to the staff is their gifts. At the last meeting she attended, the board had grown from 30 to 150. She plans to resign.

On the opposite end of the spectrum, she speaks of a wonderful experience where "great ideas don't need too much money or a lot of volunteer time. While they are not too professionally organized, I love a local housing organization where $15,000 can mobilize 150 volunteers and a house stands in a couple of weeks for a family that will buy it. Then the money is recycled. This is wonderful. The CEO is a carpenter with a heart and some organizational skills. He needs anything the board can do for him. So they just pitch in."

She concluded our conversation by saying, "I write a check because I am always traveling and serve on so many boards, but do I trust him to do the right thing? Absolutely."

Board Story

I want to help you. But open and honest communication is a must.

> *"There are all kinds of CEOs just as there are all types of board members and organizations. Some CEOs just run the place, some are start-ups where the CEO is the institution and doesn't want a strong board to get in the way. Other CEOs want the help and build a good partnership with the staff and board. I like it when the CEO is thinking and stimulating the board toward decision making. The key word is* stimulating. *If the CEO doesn't truly want the board to engage, that is no place for me. There are two sides to the handshake: the organization needs to feel it really needs me, and if it does, it must respectfully engage me in a meaningful way."*

This leader is a natural mentor, one who consistently connects the dots. She is often brought into confidential conversations for advice about interpersonal issues within an organization. One story she tells is about her relationship with a major university. She is a confidant of the president. One of the deans is new. Her university has a separate foundation to manage the funds. The newly hired foundation executive director (ED) was promised adequate staff and budget to realign the board and raise charitable funds to meet the year's goal. Once in the ED's seat, however, the dean said there was little budget and to simply please "get the job done any way you can with the people we have now."

Perplexed by the change, this ED called for help. This leader met with the ED and listened to the story (taking a day of time and four hours of driving). They agreed that the ED would set a meeting for the two of them to talk with the dean about the university's goals and how the leader could help them as a liaison with the president. The ED was to set a date within the next week. Three weeks later, the ED called this stellar leader and said she was developing a strategic plan and she would be in touch "sometime soon." No mention of the meeting with the dean. No explanation of the change of heart. This leader was willing to engage with an ED and dean she admired. Now her opinion of the ED has dropped three levels. Will she make the effort if called again? Probably not. And the ED will never know what happened.

Board Story

Board to CEO—I don't want to be an appendage.

> *"A major university with a top-flight president can run itself so they don't need much focus from me. At those [organizations] that need help, there are two models that come to mind for me. One is the strong founder CEO model and the other is the CEO who builds a strong board around him to support his cause. The latter leaves an organization so well institutionalized that if he leaves, the brain trust of the organization will go on as long as the vision is relevant."*

This leader has been on boards with very different CEOs. On one, the independent founder devoted herself full time to founding and running the organization. She was a self-motivated, capable CEO who was leading the organization toward accomplishing the mission, but she needed to be in control. "Going forward, the institution is not sustainable unless a strong board is put in place for the long term. She is good at what she does, but the board is not needed. They simply come to board meetings and listen to her reports."

On the opposite end of the spectrum, this leader works with a CEO, equally passionate about the mission but not ego-centered. This CEO has a deeply engaged board that he reaches one board member at a time. "He stays in touch frequently with every board member and is good at determining where each member is at the moment in time: working out a borrowing relationship, finding marketing partners, using political relationships, and introducing donors. Not a week passes that he doesn't feel he knows where the organization is and what he can do." This leader says, "When this kind of relationship develops, I respond when asked to do anything by the CEO."

This incredible leader is on boards from the largest foundation in the country to a small one that requires the board to do much of the heavy lifting. He has served on many search committees and looks for CEOs who are strong leaders. They may not have a strong nonprofit background, but they can engage and listen to the board. "I don't want to be an appendage," he says.

Which model will he look for next?

Board Story

When my board seat is appointed by the governor, the most important thing I want is a CEO capable of running the place.

"When the government appoints the board, the CEO must be a strong leader."

This gentleman serves on a board charged with running a $1.6 billion company, though it is a nonprofit. There are only two members there with strategy and risk experience in a broad sense. Because the board is politically beholden to some legislators, it is tied up in trivia. "The president, thank goodness, is a genius and he forces the board to deal with visionary issues. Most of these board members had to hang out at the statehouse and kiss up to all those folks to get appointed." He was appointed by the governor and didn't have to do that. He is just trying to help the president get where he wants to go. Political boards are set up for "dumbing things down." In this case, if they didn't have a brilliant, savvy president, says this board member, "the institution would be in the dark ages!"

June's Thoughts

Enthusiastic leaders love corporate boards and the CEOs with whom they serve because "the goal is clear and the CEO is held accountable." The for-profits, they say, focus on results by the CEO and board significantly more intensely than in a nonprofit. There is much joy for them in watching and learning from the nonprofit CEO who is way ahead of the board. When this happens, the admiration is palpable. Often, a strong CEO may have trouble engaging the volunteer. While board members love to see the master at work, sometimes the star at the helm leaves little room for meaningful board engagement. This scenario leads to an easy board seat except, perhaps, for giving and getting funds. "We can show up, listen to the progress, have lunch, write a check, and go home." The organization is in good hands, they say. They will be back in two months for the next report.

The "do it all" CEO is focused on the cause at hand, passionate and impatient to get the work done. Board leaders in organizations led by "lone star" CEOs admire the work so much they usually "will write the check" to support the work out of admiration for the leader. "If I thought my opinion was needed at the board meeting, I would not miss a meeting. The CEO really doesn't need us and our level of trust is high that he will get it done. The cause will be cared for. We are there as enlightened window dressing."

The downside of the CEO in control is the risk that when the CEO leaves, the organization may not be able to sustain the dynamic thrust. Or it is uncovered that maybe the board should not have trusted so much. Or, as one board leader put it, we should have "dabbled in his pie a bit more."

If the organization is undercapitalized and there is too much work for the CEO, talented board members can be mobilized to perform more staff-related work: strategic plans, financial oversight, building plans, and more. A lack of alignment comes when the cash-strapped organization is led by a top-tier CEO who still wants to "do it all." It is my experience that in the best nonprofits, the staff leaders have their egos under control and share power and make a habit of empowering both staff and boards.

There is a surge in wealthy people starting nonprofits to make societal changes that they feel are important. These are often self-funded and/or have a mission so powerful that it resonates with donors' need for transformational social change. Teach for America and the Gates Foundation are good examples. I believe the surge in social entrepreneurs is a result of lack of satisfaction in leading and giving to traditional nonprofits, many of which are viewed as cumbersome, moving too slowly for the board and staff leaders of today. And it is even more a result of the significant accumulation of wealth at ever younger years that gives people the freedom to embark upon projects that satisfy them.

We will continue to see innovative people lead imaginative nonprofits both as staff and as board members, and we will see competition escalate for excellent board and staff leaders.

The "venture" nature of the new nonprofit may well attract smart CEOs who founded a nonprofit or fund their private foundation. These venture personalities seem to want serious board and/or staff involvement. Some are finding they have to create an organization to have the level of involvement they desire. Will these potential board members play with someone else's team? What kind of CEO will they seek? Will they have patience for meetings, or will we see a dramatic change in that as well?

Differentiating the social entrepreneur from the organization he creates is often difficult. In such cases, the organization tends to collapse when the entrepreneur leaves. The real challenge for these leaders is to find a way to build a sustainable organization until the mission is met. This will take building an engaged board and staff to carry on when the organization moves from the organizing state to the governing state.

Board members said it loud and clear: In the best nonprofits, the leaders tend to be, if not exactly ego-free, people who share power and make a habit of empowering others. They cultivate a strong second-in-command, build enduring executive teams, and thoroughly engage their boards. For the CEO, this requires a significant commitment of time and creative energy to stimulate boards to engage. Even when the staff is fully capable of making all the decisions, they must create a setting for the board to be fully vested in the project at hand. It is the little things that count. The CEO must allocate time to ensure that the board has a good experience. It will come back tenfold.

Board leaders and CEOs are bringing innovation to nonprofits as never before. One big movement is to earn more money as a complement to fundraising. Mission investments, the practice of making financial investments with the intention of both furthering the mission and recovering the principal invested or earning a financial return, and micro financing (the supply of small loans, savings, and other basic financial services to the poor) are growing in popularity. "This is fun. It is brain candy," the board members say. How can the tried-and-true boards like schools and blood banks compete with this kind of excitement? So many are doing so much to solve the world's problems. Yet abandoning the basic nonprofits for the more exciting world of start-ups is not the answer.

It continues to be clear to me that seasoned board leaders, CEOs, and their senior staff must assure that best-in-class boards are supported by staff members who can create an environment for boards to drive and sustain the highest performance for their organizations and for themselves.

Board leaders who have shaped this book say emphatically that the work of the board is not something the staff does to the board. It must be something that is done with the board. Could a CPA do the work of the finance committee? Yes. Could the CEO determine the programs? Yes. Does the board distract from the business at hand? Sometimes. Are some board members not worth the effort? Yes. To be successful, though, a great CEO will be one who understands how to deeply engage the board. That is the organization that will survive and thrive beyond the current board and the CEO. Isn't that what we really want? Isn't that what our world needs?

I often remind CEOs that board members rarely get up every morning thinking about their board service. It is the strong CEO with a controlled ego that attracts and retains the best board members. It is the responsibility of the CEO and his team to create an atmosphere in which the board members are challenged and thereby given the environment where a satisfying experience is the norm. The time has come to throw a little spice into the pot and turn up the heat. But what are the right ingredients? And who is in charge of the menu?

It's About the Work, Not About the Party.

THE TRUTH

"All work and no play" makes Jack an unhappy board member.

The board meeting is a challenge. Often, there is little time for the board to understand and address issues in a thoughtful way. Barriers include schedules, agendas, and time for meaningful discussion. Productive and fulfilling board work comes when meetings are well structured with a clear call to action and, more important, when the relationship among the board and staff is solid and trust is palpable. Social occasions, good exchange in meetings, and real teamwork in committees are a few of the opportunities for board members to get to know their peers on a more personal level. When they are closer, they will begin to trust. How do we build trust? By talking and breaking bread. Listen to the truth.

Board Story

I want time to hear all opinions.

"My favorite board is one that encourages conversations to go on a little so members have time to chew on an issue. We start with adequate time and experts to educate the board on something important to the institution. For instance, what is going on with faculty? The meetings are not shorter, but they feel shorter because of the high level of participation and education."

The headmistress was facing reaccreditation in the next year. She conferred with the board chair to put the strengths and challenges of that accreditation on the agenda, taking at least 30 minutes to review the challenges with the board. She also involved faculty and staff in that presentation. Then the board had open time to fully discuss the issues, becoming better educated and making recommendations as they saw fit. What happened here? The headmistress talked openly with the board and staff about what was keeping her up at night, the faculty candidly voiced their opinions and concerns, and the board had open dialogue to satisfy their questions. All players left the meetings fully apprised of the challenges ahead and their role to resolve issues. When the accreditation team comes, the team will be prepared. Everyone knew their role. Everyone won.

Board Story

If I cannot work with my fellow board members, I cannot get to know them. If I do not know them, I cannot make change.

"An organization where the executive knows what she is doing, does it, and needs nothing from us other than money allows

no thought or dialogue. In this situation, the board has little opportunity to bond as a team. If the director can continue a quick turnover of board members, she can stay in control."

In this instance, this national organization's statewide group was given all education materials, well-defined programs, and a nationally branded event. This board member had no place to use his creativity to better the organization. The board was unable to band together to change the CEO because there was no opportunity to get to know each other outside the quarterly board meetings. So he gave his annual gift and endured his first term, declining to renew the following year citing "business demands."

Board Story

I want to do serious committee work. Work with people I get to know well.

"I actually like the committee meetings more than the board meetings. In the committees, we make strategic decisions that lead to big projects to transform the school for years to come. At board meetings, I hear talking heads. I could have just read the reports. Some boards have fallen far away from generative thinking and the exercise of meetings becomes rote. I have sailing weekends with my new friends on the board and a few of us have done business together. Formal no-talk board meetings become ungratifying."

This leader spearheaded a large-scale strategic plan for a project that would ultimately transform the school. "I was able to bring the expertise I have in my day job in finance and investments to make better decisions. I enjoy thinking through strategic questions so it was a lot of fun." This private school engaged him to chair the strategic planning committee and ultimately his family made a significant commitment in honor of his mother. His enthusiasm stemmed from the people on the committee, who he describes as bright, articulate, entrepreneurial first and focused on the mission of the school second. The committee worked hard and fast and made a real difference. The board meetings for him were less meaningful. There was little time to get to know his fellow board members as he had the committee members. Meetings were full of reports with little to no discussion. Presently, he and some of his fellow committee members are working on a new project in the community and a separate business deal.

Parents always go to PTA meetings when their children are dancing. Some things never change.

Board Story

Board to CEO—We all want the same information. Then we want to talk about it.

> *"What is a bad meeting? When you come to a meeting, get a PowerPoint presentation, are told how great everything is, and are asked to donate with no sense of involvement. Then staff pretends to listen to board members' thoughts. And, there is no chance for dialogue so I can't get to know anyone well enough to form a buddy to challenge quid pro quo. That is a bad meeting."*

This man gave his heart and soul to a small woman's college in which he believes deeply. The new president is excellent but really wants to control the message totally rather than sharing her concerns. This has created disengagement for many board members.

"We do have a new board member who is an alumna of the school and is brave enough to ask questions and take a leadership role in assuring the information is transparent. Maybe she can make a difference. I will let this term expire and get more involved in a place where I can make a real difference." So once again, meetings without discussion and decisions viewed as meaningful to the board will fast drive an excellent board member away.

This leader says, "I believe the board must assure management alignment of interest of board and the organization and run the place from the viewpoint of the stakeholder. If everyone has the same information and comes to the same decision, they are aligned. If there is disagreement, some usually have more data than others. This information sharing happens—or doesn't—in meetings. If good, transparent information is not being shared, meetings are a bust."

Board Story

Board members who fight a good fight together are friends forever.

> *"Building bonds with board and staff is far more important than being fed minutia. When bread is broken, there is a bond that begins to form. Soon you transcend to social engagement. My closest friends are board members I have worked with over the years. I would trust them with my life—and have."*

The best boards this member serves on have members geographically dispersed. They start at 4:00, have social time, and then begin dinner at 5:30. They meet early the next day and are out by noon. This allows time to set the stage for what is important in the first afternoon. The board can use that evening for casual discussion of the issues at hand or simply to get to know each other better. When a crisis comes, they stand shoulder to shoulder. She serves on one international organization's board that had a personnel disaster that was highly noted throughout the world. Because the board members knew each other very well, they were friends who were there for each other and for the organization during the crisis. They became simpatico, and fought the battle together. That was 15 years ago. And she still considers those individuals close friends.

Board Story
I want to feel appreciated.

> *"I am on some highly sophisticated boards. My favorite? A small conservation organization that is saving pristine land in the mountains. We hike together every quarterly board meeting as a part of the meeting experience. Those folks are all different. People I would never know in a million years. I love the shared passion. They even named a waterfall for me on land we saved. I love the outdoors. How could you have a better experience?"*

About 20 years ago, this leader helped start this land conservation organization. He is passionate about a lot of things: music, visual arts, and education. But the thing that has stirred the most passion is conserving the land in the mountains near his home. He told stories of hiking with his fellow board members. His ability to be "entrepreneurial and nimble" is the best thing about being involved with smaller organizations. He enjoys the social aspect of all of his involvements. "I have been the CEO of five major companies. In that role, rarely is anyone patting you on the back. Rarely does anyone appreciate what you have done, they are looking for the next thing you will do for them." In nonprofits, at least the good ones, he feels they appreciate what he is doing. He appreciates private and public ways to say thank you. He finds those occasions build friends, "whether hiking in the woods or feted at a recognition dinner."

A heartfelt "thank you" takes many forms.

Board Story

I want to know how my fellow board members think.

> *"The Freedom of Information Act has made it hard for a public body to do anything socially. That is good for transparency but it is bad for building strong teams of people who can learn to trust each other. In those groups, it is important to have retreats that build in a significant social time."*

"On one quasi-public board, we would have informal, unofficial dinners the evening before the board meeting with spouses. The staff was never invited; it was just the board and usually spearheaded by one member who was a key leader. That was a great way for us to get to know each other. It helped on that board and in many other ways, including personal business."

The group of leaders spearheading this public/private partnership was diverse geographically but focused on the economic growth of a state. There were significant environmental, real estate, and contractual issues that needed to be discussed openly and thoroughly. "Sometimes that is very difficult to do with a reporter sitting behind you when competing bids are being reviewed," said the former chairman of the organization. "We needed time to build friendship and a deep understanding of how each of us thought that each was there to move the state forward, not each person individually." A key leader made the effort to gather leaders and spouses on an informal basis. The familiarity with each member and their families made working together not only a pleasure but more effective.

June's Thoughts

Bring on the wine (or the coffee)! Board members are people—busy people, caring people, but also people who enjoy interacting with other capable folks. And a benefit they want from serving on a board is to know people who interest them and to make new friends. Sometimes those friends lead to a broader social life, other times to business relationships. Sometimes it helps get your kid into her college of choice. Sometimes it means being invited to France for a wonderful week with someone you would have never known without mutual board service.

It doesn't have to be a party. Most of the time, a party is not the best place to build friendships and trust with fellow board members. It is a committee where the board members are in charge and are challenged or given the reins to solve a problem—to think strategically. It is meetings where real learning and dialogue is encouraged. It is information that is openly shared by the staff and board members are encouraged to dig deep, to understand. It is the cocktail hour after the meeting when you find out your fellow board member went to the same school you did. It is the dinner with a small group with no presentations, just time to share. It is board work sessions with plenty of time for education and sharing thoughts. It is having the annual meeting somewhere special, probably with dinner at a board member's home. It is visiting an example of a successful project on another campus where you get to know the faculty. Sometimes it is a formal recognition at a social occasion. Other times, it is an outing that reinforces their passion for the mission. Building trust takes getting to know each other. That often happens while having fun.

My board sources tell me, however, they don't want to hang out with folks they don't admire. And admiration doesn't mean the same as "similarity." It means someone with whom they are going to have a good conversation. Good bold thinking. It may be fun or it may be learning. It just has to be good.

MYTH 6

What the Executive Committee Shares Is Its Business.

THE TRUTH

The board chair and the CEO must build trust with the entire board.

When a CEO and a board chair, in particular, have experience and wisdom coupled with true passion for the cause, a joint vision can be shared. This shared relationship, it seems, is built on trust and transparency. The confident CEO will welcome questions by the board. The confident board chair will trust the board with information and encourage open dialogue at any time. The truth is not held by the executive committee only. Hear what our seasoned leaders had to say about trust. Listen to the truth.

Board Story

When a lack of trust exists between staff and board, board will side with board most of the time.

> *"A person I have the highest regard for was ruthlessly maligned by the president of our college for questioning his*

reports. He was doing his job as a board member of resisting generic PowerPoint presentations and thinking about the repercussions of what the numbers meant. He and I both resigned. I have zero tolerance for violation of basic ethics."

The executive committee of this college board of trustees was a dream team. All in high-profile careers, they were the "poster children" for board influence and affluence. They applauded the addition of a talented chief financial officer (CFO) to the administrative team who was "very sharp about the finances of this higher education institution." The committee and the CFO met frequently because of financial issues facing the school. "We were getting pabulum from the president. When we directly asked the CFO about the issues, we felt he was intelligent, honest, and straightforward. So I, as chairman, asked our most savvy financial board member to dig into the situation with the CFO, and he did. The situation turned out to be voodoo economics," said this board chairman. Further, it became clear to the committee that the president was projecting manufactured numbers and expecting the committee to accept his report. The members understood that sometimes you have to "rob Peter to pay Paul" but they quickly discovered that the president was being untruthful. Another wrinkle to the story was the membership of the board, which also had a high percentage of ministers and bishops who were swayed by the "hail fellow, well met" personality of the president because they were interested in his programs much more than the financial integrity of the school.

The committee had evidence of lack of transparency, even dishonesty, with the board so they "called his hand" on the issue. "We met with the president and worked out a face-saving way for him to resign and he agreed. Next was a called board meeting out of town where all board members were either present or on the telephone. Between the agreement to resign and the board meeting, the president had a change of heart and went to his buddies on the board misrepresenting the true situation. Quickly, the board took sides. "We had not counted the votes before the meeting. The board rejected our accusations. All members of the executive committee resigned that day." Six months later, the remaining board members fired the president, realizing that he had been dishonest all along.

I asked what they had learned from the experience? "Count your votes first before ever going into a meeting," he said and laughed. "Actually, the real lesson learned is that doing the right thing can often be hard. The truth always wins."

Board Story

I want to be your best advocate if you fully explain the issue.

> *"If you are on the board and not getting the full picture on financials or human relations issues, you need to leave the board or take action with the CEO."*

As the chair of a statewide organization, the board was clearly not getting the complete picture. "We continually asked for information to clarify our questions and could not get it. We asked for an independent audit and got it. The information led to the release of the CEO. If the CEO cares and is passionate and totally honest with the board at all times, almost anything can be worked out. In this situation, the CEO caused himself irrevocable harm with a simple lack of transparency. He felt passionately about driving programs that were too expensive for our budget. He did not personally benefit but he was not transparent with the board and that got him into a bind."

She goes on to say, “So many CEOs really don’t want constructive criticism.” The president of her favorite college board welcomes it with open arms. He wants the board to think deeply and critically and help him avoid pitfalls. For example, at one point the general education curriculum was due for review.

“Students were required to take a number of non-degree-specific courses, leaving some to feel that requirement left too few hours to train students deeply in their chosen subjects. Some faculty, alumni, and friends of the college were upset with the idea that traditional courses may be reduced.”

Because this president had fully educated the board about the issues, and because the “president is a wonderful communicator and comfortable in his own skin, the board stood firmly by his side and helped him weather the storm and do what was best for the students and the college. In the end, the board and all constituencies trusted the president even more.

Board Story

I want the board to trust me. I have to say things out loud.

“I came onto a board in chaos. A financial decision split the board and half resigned. Most who resigned were long-time local residents. Our headmaster was retiring and we had a horrible public relations disaster from an incident years ago. The board then selected the next headmaster who was a high-profile former college president. At the last minute, the chosen candidate and board determined that it was not the right fit. This, too, was another high-profile incident. Thank goodness, we brought in an interim who was revered by the community and the board. She taught me how to move most decisions out of the executive committee and how to build a totally transparent organization. Today, we function at the highest level.”

She was new to the board and was viewed as a board member with the wisdom to navigate choppy waters. Paired with a highly seasoned interim head of school, the two started the process of healing. They brought in a consultant to help the board learn about the next level of thinking and helped them grow from operational to strategic to generative thinking. They worked through case studies to practice generative thinking. They began to meld the vision of the head and the board. She found that the head of school taught her to know when it was appropriate to talk to a staff person directly rather than having to go through the head every time. She learned to touch base frequently with all board members to ensure that everyone knew what was going on even if they were not heavily involved. And she learned that if she made a mistake to admit it out loud in front of the entire board. "They will forgive you if you are totally transparent," she said. "Today, the school and the board are together, with one shared vision. The board comes to the table with both wisdom and work and have no egos attached. They are there to help, to make things great."

This is a board of twenty-nine members. Each person on the board knows all the details of any decision requiring board feedback. All opinions are welcome. Board attendance is nearly 100%.

Board Story

I want to be engaged. Too strong an executive committee makes me feel like a bystander.

> *"I enjoy being the chairman and sitting on the executive committee with a strong staff leader beside me. With this small group, I can accomplish important tasks. I have to do these jobs well because I am not only representing myself but my company. I know the rest of the board has a hard time getting*

engaged and feel far away from the decision-making core. Personally, I hated this board when I was out of the inner circle, so I know how they feel."

The statewide chamber of commerce is a powerful group in his state. By virtue of being the president of his company, he is placed in positions of power and now chairs the organization. The chairman position turns over every year, which creates a very strong staff-led program. There are 50 members of this board so most decisions are made at the executive committee level. It is here that significant policy decisions are made, which are critical to the vibrancy of the business communities, particularly in the arena of advocacy. This leader has been on both sides of the fence: on the executive committee and not. "No question that being in the circle of leadership is more fun. I wish I could solve this issue, but I just don't know how," he said.

Strong Executive Committees are a great way to engage 10 percent of the board. Too bad about the other 90 percent!

Board Story

I want the executive committee to be used only in critical situations.

"I have ended up on the executive committee of every board on which I have sat. By the time I reach that level, I am usually very engaged or I will have left the board by then. For years I have been thinking about how misused executive committees are, often populated with power brokers on the board who like to hold things close to the vest."

This woman is currently chairing a community foundation and the board is composed of very wise people. Clearly, any member of the board could be chairman and do a wonderful job. They are now fully endowed, much because of the quality of leadership over the years. Discussions are thoughtful and deeply meaningful to their community.

How can you justify a community endowment of $200 million unless the work of the board and staff is totally transparent and focused on the mission and not the individuals? This year she suggested, and the board has agreed, that the executive committee will be used only in emergencies. There will be no private, unilateral decisions made on this board. The board meetings are now meaty and everyone feels that they have achieved involvement and understanding by each member of the board. The board rarely misses a meeting, a social occasion, a site visit, or anything else the organization needs them to do. "Why?" she asked. "Because we seek the thoughts of each member and value their time and wisdom, and they see that we are listening."

June's Thoughts

Times have changed.

I remember the time I kept the change from an errand my father asked me to run. Several days later he asked me about the change and I said, "I assumed you didn't want it back since you didn't ask." If you are a Boomer like me, you can imagine what that assumption meant to my dad. Let's just say, to this day, I do not assume that someone wants me to keep something that is theirs. Board members, I believe, think that any information about the work, politics, challenges, and anything else about their organization is theirs. They are responsible. It belongs to them, right?

Every piece of literature about boards says that if the organization is in trouble, it is the whole board that gets in trouble.

It is not just the executive committee. Is there any wonder, then, that boards feel not only the desire but the need to have a clear picture of the scene in their organization at any given time?

Believe me, I know from my work as CEO, consultant, and board member that the fewer people who have to be consulted to make a decision, the easier it is. But is our work supposed to be easy? Are only a few to hold the knowledge? How did we get to this place?

I believe that we must take a good, hard look at an organization in total. Yep, all of it. The whole enchilada. Here is the bottom line for me with boards: If you do not trust your members with all of the information necessary to fully understand the issues, then you have recruited the wrong board.

When board members feel left out, heaven help you with getting them to act. Often, the scenario looks like this: "Listen, we will call you when we need you, we will ask for your opinion when we need it, but fact is, there are a few powerful folks who can run this show and you are window dressing. So, listen up, just don't ask too many questions and you can continue to play with us. And, if you are really, really good, someday, you might get to know stuff that the big girls and boys on the Executive Committee know. Maybe."

Common sense says, and our board members confirm, that there is a better way.

It takes time and patience to deal with others. Your spouse, your children, your business partners. . . . Wouldn't it just be easier sometimes to have a separate credit card and order what you want? Sure, it would. Is that the strongest partnership?

The simple answer: A board is a group of people chosen to make strategic decisions for an organization. That is the definition. It does not say a chosen few are to make the decisions. It says the board decides. If the board is to think in a transformational way, they must have enough information. A board with wisdom and the opportunity to exercise that level of thinking will be a board that will bond.

The use of committees or task forces to vet an issue remains viable at the point of the entire board making a decision; however, the board needs to be fully educated with enough time to consider an issue before the vote is taken.

So what's the problem here? From my vantage point, it is with the makeup of the board chosen in haste and just to fill the numbers, to check the boxes. Does each board member have wisdom and character? If so, it really doesn't matter how many there are if there is trust. And trust comes with knowledge.

Great Board Members = Big Check Writers. That's All.

THE TRUTH

Board giving is directly correlated to the board experience.

You know the game: "Look, you said yes to this board seat, and we need money to operate. We are, after all, a not-for-profit! We need the annual fund to pay salaries, benefits, electricity, rent"—you know, that kind of thing. Gets you excited, doesn't it? Our board leaders tell me that fundraising is the last reason they want to be on a board. They know their organization needs their money and their connections to others. But it is the meaningful experience with the organization and its CEO and fellow board members that stirs their passion and is the precursor to joyfully given gifts. If you want your board member to stretch to give, it is quite simply about their experience. Listen to the truth.

Board Story

I want to lead. Then I will want to give.

> *"I have served on several community boards just to be a good citizen. I did not make a difference. I was just filling a seat.*

On the other hand, I was asked to serve on a college board that was pretty weak but had a new and strong president. He asked me to gather the best board I could recruit and help him find the funds to make the school excel. I am thrilled to be a part of this change, and I have recruited a powerful international board and given and raised millions to help him get there. Now, that is fun!"

In this case, the board needed to be changed to reach the level of leadership and giving necessary to be successful, and this board member was given full permission to choose and recruit the board they needed to be successful. Seven world-wide board members later, the school's budget and programs are aligned and $60 million has been contributed to the school. Why was this fun for the board member? He was able to use his skills, friends, and position to really make a difference. What allowed that to happen?

"The president was conscious of what he didn't know and could not do and used the board to fill in the gaps." What did that require? One brave president. One dedicated board member. What else did the board member do? He gave them a million dollars. This was not, by the way, his alma mater!

Board Story
I want personal satisfaction.

"Let's get real here. If I weren't rich, I wouldn't be sought after as a board member. Years ago, I was young and more easily impressed. The chair of a big bank in Chicago called me personally and invited me to serve on my college board. I was honored to be asked. He showed me he really wanted me

> *by going out of his way to meet my schedule in my place. I knew even then that significant giving was part of the game, so early on I started making annual gifts of note. At 55 now, I made the largest gift I have ever made to the college when I chaired the capital campaign. Later, I became the board chair. I made my swan-song gift and made a real effort to get others to do so, too. I started out with charity and ended up with philanthropy. In the end, I was setting an example. Today, I spend time and money where I feel I can make the biggest difference."*

This wonderful and energetic philanthropist says he is "listed" on an international religious board to which he feels an obligation. It is all about fundraising with no attention to mission. He doesn't even go to the meetings because they are all social. "Each name is trying to be bigger than the next." Once a year, he puts up with the development officer coming to visit and asking for an ever-increasing gift. "I give them more than I would if they didn't come." Is it charity or philanthropy? Neither, he says. "It is just an obligation."

The most satisfying board experience for this nonprofit leader is a camp for sick kids. This was not a "buttoned up" organization, but "a few fellow leaders met the challenges, worked hard, and gave big to build the camp. It was a start-up with little money and a board that had a bunch of names."

But he, along with those of his fellow leaders who could, gave big bucks in relation to the organization's scope. They just did it. Now it works and is a great camp doing a great service for really sick kids. "This is normally an organization I would write a $1,000 check to, but I have done and probably will continue to do much more because I just find it personally satisfying."

Board Story

I want only the CEO and board member at the meeting.

> *"In a for-profit institution, the fiduciary responsibility is so highly defined, staff members understand the board has a responsibility to probe, to dig in. In the nonprofit, this understanding is not as well established. If I cannot dig in, being on a board is a waste of my time. I have other things to do with my time if it is not highly valued."*

This high-level corporate leader finds that nonprofit staffs rarely understand that the board cannot do their duty if they do not clearly understand the finances and the operations of the organization. Nonprofits seem opaque to him.

"The level of reporting just isn't enough to keep one engaged. Organizations with large staffs and boards are the most difficult." The large-staff-driven programs he has been involved with want to keep boards quiet.

"With 30 people in a room, especially those who bring a lot of staff to the board meetings, it is practically impossible to ask more than one question. When asked, it generally takes four or five more questions to get close to a genuine answer. If you multiply that by 30, he feels it is impossible to dig deeply into anything without feeling you are monopolizing the conversation." His large organization runs the board like it is more about the process than the results, he says.

He prefers boards that are 10 or fewer members and populated with strong, intelligent people with relevant experience needed for the issue at hand. "A small group provides a great opportunity to have meaningful discussion. No one but the CEO should be with the board at a meeting. Having too many staff members stifles discussion."

While the board is more than 10 strong, he and his fellow board members have become deeply engaged in strategic decisions. Those decisions have led to the need for additional significant endowment monies.

He now chairs the capital campaign. Why? He believes in the cause and because he has made a real difference in the way the organization is run. He now trusts it. He can look to his left and to his right and know he has a great board leader/giver on either side.

Board Story
I want bold action.

> *"The president and I understood that this small, highly diverse university had to change to survive. I had never been involved there. I was asked by the president to advise him how to transform the school. Together, we changed the board and the program. I wrote a check because I believed in the institution."*

The president of this troubled university had a vision of how to transform the student experience but he knew he did not have the leadership surrounding him to make it happen. He gave carte blanche to this national leader to head a committee to examine the school and give him direction for the most effective use of funds and plans to transform the school. National leaders were attracted to this challenge. Many have transitioned to the board, now made up of some of the best and brightest. "The meetings are electric, and the action is bold."

For instance, the board analysis recommended doing away with the football program. The president felt the alumni would rebel. The board said that if they want the program, they have to pay for it. The football program was canceled. "We gave them tough love." They examined the quality of the academic programs and the number of students enrolled. If either the enrollment was low or the program was not of high quality, the program was eliminated. Now the programs are more focused, the university knows what it is good at, and the students know where to go for selected majors. The school is running in the black and admissions are up. Why did this work?

"The president knew he needed help; he reached out beyond the normal constituency and took the advice." Quite simply, this is another example of a top-tier board member being attracted to a midsize organization that needed serious help. It was not the glitz appointment that attracted the leaders. It was a sincere CEO who was transparent enough with his situation to let "doers" in. They found the experience like a great burger and good bottle of wine. They lapped it up and left the university better for it. Their brains and their money were given freely.

"Believe me, I can write checks, but that is the last reason I want to be on the board."

Board Story

I want the president to make fundraising calls with me. If he wants my money, he will.

> *"Now that I am a high-net-worth person, I can get the seven- and eight-figure gifts. This cannot be done by anyone other than the president, nor could it have been done by me when I was 40. And for me to function well, I cannot be subjected to board meetings that make me crabby."*

A self-made man, he has little patience for hesitation in decisions and action. He says there is no way a nonprofit board can be as stimulating as venture capital endeavors. Why? "The amount of pressure that is brought to bear by nonprofits that need dollars is amazing. These groups are in two camps: those that need the dollars but aren't going to take your advice or do what they need to, and those that have a dynamic leader who wants the dollars and tells you to go get them and you say 'yes sir.'" It seems to this board member that the organizations are always looking to boards to fix problems. He resigns from needy organizations and gravitates to excellent ones. He further suggests that "running a business is not as complicated as serving as a college president, who must wear many hats, including that of the chief development officer."

"I admire the VP of advancement, but he cannot pull off the eight-figure gifts; that takes the president and a volunteer who has done the same." All of this work takes meetings to define the plan. "I tend to be a loner in many ways and do my own thing. I have trouble on nonprofit boards because I get bored easily. If I cannot make an impact quickly, I find myself getting really crabby. Plus, I have no tolerance for pontification, which seems to be prevalent in nonprofit boardrooms." For this very generous philanthropist, it well may be better for the president to work with him one on one. The institution and the board member will both get what they want that way.

Board Story

I want to build my team, my way. Then you will get my money.

> *"At this stage of my life, I serve only where I can make a difference. So that means for me, I like to start up organizations. I get the message down, get the passion going, and build the right team, and the money follows. It's easy, really."*

This much-sought-after woman has started numerous organizations, including her businesses. She likes to take an idea and then be left to set it up and find the right person to run the organization. She likes being given full responsibility to gather the board and set the agenda. "When you have the freedom of structuring well, have your personal choice of staff, and control the purse strings, then you can control policy. When like-minded people are gathered for a meeting around an exciting idea, the sparks fly and great things get done. It is when things get too bureaucratic that it gets dull. That's when it is time for me to leave."

For this leader, the energy around a start-up produces meetings with much to be accomplished in a short time. There is no problem with dialogue and action at this stage of the game. Nor is there a problem of a gift commensurate with the involvement.

Board Story

I want to bring my significant corporate money to organizations that are very, very good.

> *"My arts organization is a fun learning experience, but my college boards have long-term impact. I like both. On boards, there are money spenders and money savers. On arts boards, the artistic love the arts and they tend to be more willing to spend. Then there are savers. The savers are a very different cast of characters and both together make a very interesting opportunity. I get to look deep into the soul of the organization. When it is very, very good, I bring significant corporate money to the table."*

On both boards this leader was able to bring creative financing to the table because of his knowledge of the marketplace. On a board, everyone brings something special to the table. "Mine is financial: how to invest an endowment so it can grow." On one college board, he helped found a real estate foundation; they built student housing and knew how to get that done. On another college board, they don't have the high-level staff to manage these processes but that was okay with him because they needed his advice, have taken it, and then have staff that can follow through. "I like that I am needed." With each of these organizations, his particular talent is invited, he is engaged in making "the deal" happen, and that feels good. He is valued.

As a corporate leader, he can guide the destination of corporate money if he feels passionate about the work. And on the ones he enjoys the most, he and his wife make significant contributions as well.

June's Thoughts

At the beginning of this book, I said something we all know. What we need to do with board members is simple to say, yet difficult to do. It's just as simple to say, "Don't eat anything white and you will be beautiful forever!" But how difficult it is to do just that every day. How does a busy CEO have time to find the right place for every board member to deeply engage in a meaningful way? How many times can we ask a committee to revisit finance policy and relationships? For certain, using board members' talents consistently well is a challenge for any staff. Managing board member relationships is not only time consuming but delicate.

Here Is the Real Truth: You Just Have to Do It

Here is some advice my clients know only too well: The relationship you have with your board will make or break you. What you do with them is your most important work. CEOs seem to fall into two camps: one with significant resources to run and fund the organization with staff, and another whose CEO has few resources and must be astute enough to engage the board to do real work in addition to real thinking. There are challenges for both. Even those with extensive resources who have the staff to do the work must be willing to allow the board to dig deep into issue and bring their best ideas to solutions. Sometimes excellent CEOs have few resources. Here, the opportunity for board engagement is huge. The challenge is to carve the time and build the trust to let the board do some heavy lifting.

Regardless of the situation, it is the CEO's responsibility to personally allocate time for thoughtful board management or delegate that to appropriate staff. I work with nonprofits every day. Much of my work is focused on meeting a fundraising goal. One of our consultants calls it "philductivity," the forcing of philanthropy within the third quarter of the year.

This is the problem with fundraising as structured in the vast majority of organizations. Administration has a priority project. Development has a goal to meet in order to fund the project. And always, that goal is to increase each year. Right? Campaign-planning studies measure the readiness to give to the project. But the prediction of success—or not—is based on donor readiness to give at the needed amounts.

Donors and board members are ready to give at the needed amounts only if they have had a *meaningful experience* with the organization that is asking. By now you have listened to the tribe; you have heard our board member experiences.

Is your board ready? Right now?

In too many situations, we have exactly six months to get the potential donor or board member from "We are building a new building and it will cost $181 million" to "George, we would like you to consider a gift of $10 million." Ever been there? I have, and so have most of our board advisors for this book.

What they are saying to you is this: If the project has my fingerprints all over it, if you really let me as a board member use what I know to help you transform the organization, I will want to give you money and help you get the rest of it. But, Buddy, it well may not be in your fiscal year. It will be in my time when I am ready. And it is all about my experience with you along the way.

Far too many staff, donors, and board members experience philductivity. I believe this is partially driving board members and donors to more entrepreneurial nonprofit work. Motivated by growing competition to attract donor dollars, charities are going beyond our long-standing practices. Some are adopting innovative investment strategies or owning other ventures outright. This fits right in with what you have heard from our board leaders: It is so much more fun to work with a great corporate board. If we are not careful, the traditional nonprofit will lose boards and donors to a small but budding practice—what some label the fourth sector—composed of organizations driven by both social purpose and financial promise that fall somewhere between traditional companies and charities. Stephanie Strom of the *New York Times* writes,[1] "The term 'fourth sector' derives from the fact that participants are creating hybrid organizations distinct from those operating in the government, business, and nonprofit sectors." Consumers, employees, managers, and—perhaps most important—investors are driving the phenomenon.

Another threat to traditional charities is venture philanthropists who are excited to donate their time, leadership expertise, and money. The socially minded entrepreneur takes his private-sector skills and applies them to solving a social problem. Generations of a family, for example, may use their wealth created by the older to satisfy the desires to change the world of the

---

[1] Stephanie Strom, "Businesses Try to Make Money and Save the World," *The New York Times*, May 6, 2007.

young. This looks like a profile of most board leaders in this book. They are seeking ventures in their traditional nonprofits. One more time: It is about their experience!

One of our consultants has recently completed the first land grant university campaign to raise over $1 billion. He frequently talks about "30 being the new 50." He is referring to young, well-educated graduates who are not satisfied with going to work for a normal corporation because they are passionate about doing good in the world and doing it in business. And there is a whole generation of people who've become extraordinarily wealthy very early in life and are now asking themselves if they can create change in the world. Do we believe that we can do business as usual with these leaders? Do we believe we can continue to extract funds from those who are fortunate enough to have them without engaging their thoughts?

No. We must revolutionize the board and donor experience—that is, if you want their leadership and largesse.

The new type of philanthropist requires fresh, more sophisticated ways to engage. Wealthy baby boomers have been and will be contributing the lion's share of charitable giving. As this group passes through, we have seen an entire industry develop to give more strategically. We believe the social entrepreneurs have become bored with the more traditional nonprofit in which decisions are slow and methodical. Hundreds of innovative nonprofits and foundations are on a march to allow donors to be more entrepreneurial in their giving and working. If the traditional nonprofits sit still, fundraisers will be ill-equipped to chase money. For sure, we see more innovation on the way.

While any giving is good giving, there is a difference between charity and philanthropy—beyond the size of the donation. Charity provides relief to an immediate situation, such as sending $50 to help the local telethon or making a $1,000 annual contribution. Philanthropy is a long-term commitment—and investment—in a cause. Commitment comes when a trusting relationship exists with the leadership of an organization. Again, it is a good experience that grows a relationship from a charitable level to the much higher philanthropic one. A philanthropist identifies with a cause, learns about the issues, tracks how his investment is being used and is involved throughout the process.

Stroke the brain and the board member will stroke the check.

Philanthropy is practiced by those who trust the organizations in which they are fully engaged.

No One Cares About Gift Expectations Two Years Out.

THE TRUTH

Tell the board in advance what is expected—all of it.

Any seasoned board member understands that a nonprofit needs contributions to do their work. The CEO who invests time to educate and engage a potential board member will have a leg up every time. Excitement for a project or a cause often does not take a long time. The length of time is directly proportionate to the alignment of the organization with the recruit's interests and capacity. So, when it is time to invite leaders to serve, take the time to educate them about the institution. Take the time to build a relationship. Take the time for them get to know the leaders. And before asking them to join you, tell them all of it. Why the movement is important and what it will take to achieve the mission. Go ahead. Tell them all of it. If they still say yes, you will have good leaders. Listen to the truth.

Board Story

I don't want to work with the uninitiated.

> *"If you are bringing me in because you are launching a campaign, tell me up front. Also, don't let me come on a board where the other members are unsophisticated about what it takes to achieve the organization's fundraising goals. For heaven's sake, don't get me on a board that doesn't even understand a giving pyramid. You are not going to raise big bucks at a cocktail party."*

This was yet another story about a seasoned board member totally surprised at joining a board with the "right names" but, in the attempt to develop a campaign strategy, discovered most of the board members wanted to throw a party rather than have meaningful face-to-face meetings with potential donors capable of making significant gifts. This relates to our AlignMint™ theory: Bring together board members of similar sophistication in the "giving and getting" arena. Top-tier board members do not want to review fundraising 101 with their fellow members. At minimum, segment the group. "I do not understand a CEO painting an untrue portrait of the organization to me. I now ask a lot of questions about the board and their engagement . . . and that means giving. I just don't have the patience anymore for leaders pretending they are not going into a big campaign when they are." This board leader actually likes campaigns, and he won't run away from a big challenge. As a matter of fact, he will run away from a little one. A tennis pro doesn't gain much from playing with someone who just picked up a racquet for the first time. The same is true for a seasoned board member.

Board Story
I want to know what is expected of me.

> *"Those who recruit should be more up front, open, and honest with businesspeople representing a company. We have budgets to which we must adhere. Far too often, we are told a minimum commitment of dollars that is expected only to later find that something much greater is being asked. We don't want to be embarrassed by not being able to meet the challenge. That means we either suffer embarrassment or make it up personally. We don't like that, and it is not fair. I know the higher profile the board, the higher the expected giving, the more I as a corporate leader am likely to give personally. The people of the organization are more aligned—a good fit."*

"I hear the board recruiters talking about 'playing down' the giving part of the board experience all the time. They also play down the expectations of board work." It is so easy to flatter someone about how much you need their thoughts when what organizations need most is their money. Corporations are on the strategy bandwagon that most foundations began long ago. "Here is the reality: More money is available to fewer organizations as companies want to make strategic decisions about their giving," he said. This means that corporate leaders need to plan their involvement carefully.

At Corporate DevelopMint, we have developed a process to build win-win relationships with our clients' corporate and business partners: BizDevelopMint™. We developed it because this is such a challenging task but has so much potential. This corporate leader understands the need for him, as a board leader, to belong to boards that complement the work of his company if the board seat is a company one. These business-savvy leaders want to know very clearly how their business can have a mutually satisfying experience from his board position. Certainly, those business leaders you recruit need a clear understanding of what you want from them in every way: what job you want them to do and what funding you want them to consider. Tell them up front. Be transparent, too, about what they will get from you.

Board Story

I want you to honor what I tell you about our corporate giving policy.

> *"In many cases, I am so consumed by work that serving on boards gets me out, and I like that. I like providing third-party oversight to guide a positive future. However, I will tell you that I am now a stickler for digging deeply into what a nonprofit really expects of me. I find that even the largest and most sophisticated organization will hedge when I ask that question. I want the leadership to be very clear about what they are asking me to do. How do they see me participating? I now interview them well enough to see if they want my engagement—not just my money. If they do not want my brain, then I don't want to serve."*

This corporate philanthropy leader is often asked to take board seats, even though she is young. In the beginning, she would accept, explain the company's giving policies up front, and elaborate on her skills in public relations and marketing. She felt that she was very clear about the range of giving that was possible, the role she could play, and that her giving would be from corporate. All too often, these organizations would come back to her the following year and ask for a personal contribution as well as an over-the-top ask from corporate. Rarely was she asked to get involved in heightening the visibility, a place where she felt she could make a significant difference. Today, she calls current board members to ask about their experience on the board before accepting. And she finds employees to serve on boards that do not personally interest her.

June's Thoughts

Let us remember that the best of board leaders want to get their hands dirty, to really make a difference, and to use their talents and their relationships to create something wonderful. They want lasting results. They are not afraid of a challenge; in fact, they embrace one! Also, remember that the last reason they want to be invited is to give you money.

These leaders know that you want their money. You will get it when they respect their fellow board members, have a passion for the mission, respect and like the CEO, and are challenged to aid the organization in doing meaningful work.

Transparent means clear, open, honest. Our leaders like to think big, so a capital campaign, if that is in alignment with the future of the organization, will not frighten a top-tier board leader. The board leader is often looking carefully at the professional staff: Can they sacrifice their own needs to the greater ambition of something larger and more lasting than themselves? If the "next step" for the organization is to boost the fame, power, and admiration of the CEO, they will most likely be turned off. They will be suspicious of what they are being told the organization's future is. However, if the CEO is focused on what he or she can inspire the organization to build, create, and really contribute to making the world a better place, then it is possible for that leader, partnered with board leaders focused on the mission and not their own ego, to be open and thoroughly honest in the recruitment process.

If the organization is completely aligned, they tell the recruits what is required of them. Listen carefully and probe to understand what they want. Is this right for them? Can they find their passion? If the organization is not totally aligned, potential recruits should know that, too. Ask them to help you get there. It seems to me that not one of these leaders would back off from too big a challenge if they can find the passion. They would, however, back off from a team with the wrong reasons for being on board.

I am guilty of manipulating leaders by getting the right people to ask them—people to whom it is almost impossible to say no. "Just get them on, then we will warm them up." Let us all pledge to change the way we do this. Let us pledge to take the time with as many visits as it takes to get them involved, to have them ready to make an investment. I promise you I will do that. Will you?

Boards Get a Lot from Training.

THE TRUTH

Board members hate anything labeled training.

When I asked board members if any training sessions have ever been meaningful to them, most became silent. They put their hands on their heads to think and were silent for minutes—long, painful minutes. (As a board trainer myself, I tried not to take this too personally!) Then they all said, "No, not really." Crushed, I probed a little deeper.

There I learned the problem.

Never call it *training*. These elite board members love learning—learning about the industry trends of their organizations, about best practices and benchmarking, and yes, even fundraising if it is *very* specific to their situation, their cause. But call it *training* and you've lost them before the coffee's even been served.

Listen to the truth.

Board Story

I want you to educate me.

Silence. More silence.

"No, I cannot think of a board training that was meaningful." I heard this statement more than 50 times.

"A consultant once came to the board work session and walked us through the four factors that we, as board members, must understand if our college is to grow and prosper. I had never heard this information before in this way. I have now developed my personal measure so that I can better measure our success. Was this board training? It didn't feel like that. It felt like insider information, a good educational board experience."

"I was the first noncorporate, non jet-owning chair of a huge, national human services organization. As we faced a media fire, a past chairman and one of the most successful corporate leaders in the world asked if I had ever had intensive media training. I had not. His company paid for me to spend an excruciating week in training. This was one of the most valuable experiences of my life. I will be forever grateful. I was able to help my organization because of that training. Was it specific training to be a better board member? No. It did, however, help me be a better leader and save the organization during a very tough time."

These are the types of responses I heard when I asked what I thought was a simple question about training. Essentially, these well-respected and intelligent people don't want to be preached to or feel like they are being forced to swallow the newest theory or mantra. Instead, they want to be educated, to be shown a tool that is complementary to their existing skill set.

For many—who may not consider themselves natural fundraisers—this means learning that fundraising isn't simply asking their friends for money. There is a method, a routine, a tested script that tells a compelling story. Sometimes, all that board members need is a little education in how to find their own storytelling voice.

While it may be sold as "training" by a consulting firm or a CEO, it must be couched as brain candy for the board.

Board Story

I want to be educated about your issues long before you ask me to join the board.

> *"I went on boards immediately out of college because of our family foundation. We know that a large percentage of our gifts may not change the world, but we hope it makes a difference in some way, large or small. I like to help give and raise money and spend my life doing that. The difference now and when I got started is that I know how to find the fit between me and the organization. I want the organization to be able to be clear about what they can do and, more important, how it may impact systemic problems. I call this educating a donor. For good education to occur, the board member visiting me must be able to tell me the story. That takes training."*

As the head of a family foundation, this leader has spent the last 30 years thinking about nonprofits on a daily basis. When I asked him about good presentations from a nonprofit, his answer was in no way surprising. "Very few staff and board leaders can walk in and tell me in five minutes what they want and what difference it will make," he says. When I asked what it takes to have an articulate presentation, he simply said, "Training."

Yes, the board and staff must be trained and must practice making an articulate, convincing presentation.

I was shocked at how many contributors said the same thing: "It feels so much better when an organization makes a well-prepared, well-thought-out plan for the organization. Do they clearly articulate the issue they are trying to impact, or are they dancing around the issue?" For this board member, the major environmental organizations in the country are doing a good job of this today. Instead of fighting against so much, today they are bringing solutions to the issues. The past 50 years of educating the population about climate change has begun to take effect. "My point is that early education about the case, long before becoming a donor or a board member, will prevent any surprise of the need for significant philanthropy. We must help people understand before we ask them to do something.

June's Thoughts

Throughout the stories in this book are woven experiences that could be construed as training. The meaningful encounters with a CEO, a fellow board member, and consultants, in a very real sense, were training. The board member who serves on many search committees is there because of his wisdom, I suspect. He refers to a consultant who made the point that most nonprofit organizations are not prepared to handle a top-flight CEO. They are not prepared to pay them well enough and engage with them on a mutually satisfying journey. Their board is constantly changing and so is their boss. This was training. A knowledgeable consultant made and validated a point to this board member. He internalized this information and used it to help change the organization to better handle the next CEO.

Another board member, one of the finest chairpersons I have ever witnessed, was also "trained." She, too, says she was put in the position of chairman because of her healing style of management and wisdom to bring unity to a divided board. She was coached by a very wise interim CEO, who helped her learn when, as the board chair, it was appropriate to talk directly to staff and when it was not. She also welcomed the case method teaching by a consultant in which the board had to think through situations and make decisions. Those decisions were fully vetted in a safe environment throughout a day of training. But because it was specific and meaty, it was a learning experience, a hands-on, participative experience, so it did not feel like training. It felt like education, like a good experience.

I have learned and am glad to share how important it is to design learning experiences appropriate to the current viability of the organization juxtaposed with the wants and level of experience of the staff and board. That board education must not be generic (except with the totally uninitiated board member). Each board member's skills and experience must be well understood by the CEO so that he or she can be brought up to speed and shine among peers, not be embarrassed by a lack of knowledge or experience.

Let us lose the word *training* and take up the word the tribe likes: *experience*. A good learning experience.

The Other Side of the Story

Throughout the interview process, there were several professional staff leaders mentioned by these elite board members. I was curious about how they provided their boards with a good experience and if their thoughts and lessons mirrored what I have learned through this research.

Jon Dellandrea, PhD, Former Pro Vice Chancellor, The University of Oxford

Dr. Jon Dellandrea is Canadian and one of world's most successful university advancement professionals, having excelled in every place he has led development efforts. He was an early leader in multimillion-dollar campaigns and never looked back, later hitting the billion-dollar mark before it was commonplace among elite universities. At this writing, he is back in Canada after heading up development and external affairs as the pro-vice-chancellor at the University of Oxford in Canada. He broke fundraising records as the vice president and chief advancement officer at the University of Toronto, where he also served as the president of the University of Toronto Foundation, and held faculty positions in the Rotman School of Management and in the Division of Management and Economics. Earlier, he was with the University of Waterloo and president of the Mount Sinai Foundation. Does that make you want to listen to what he has to say? Here goes.

Jon said very succinctly, "There is a delicate balance between governance and management that works most successfully when total transparency is present—playing poker with the cards face up. In every situation, I have an ironclad commitment that there will be no surprises to my board leaders, and I never waste their time."

I asked Jon what he believes makes the best experience for the board. Listen to the truth:

He believes that the best leaders are attracted to "highly respected and highly impactful institutions where board members feel a deep sense of personal pride and ownership of that organization. The organization, though it may be large and complex, provides concrete ways for the board or committee members to become deeply engaged and involved in such a way that they feel a deep personal reward."

How does he provide this? Jon develops with his staff a thorough strategic plan with clear and measurable goals. At the first of the year, he takes that plan to the committee and details the work to be done and who is responsible. The committee is asked for their advice and thoughts on making the organization better. Then, several times a year, the plan and movement on that plan is brought back to the committee. The reports are always an unvarnished truth, totally transparent.

The chair of the committee is met with frequently. If there are issues, all of them are explained clearly, with solutions suggested. Then the chair is asked, "What do you think?" If there is a true partnership, if there is a spirit of "we are in this together for the best of the university" then everything works out. The chair then is prepared to work with other board or committee members with no concern for being caught without proper information. What results? Trust. Trust that the truth will always be told.

Jon's large organizations are mostly staff-driven but with the understanding that there are times that only a volunteer can make relationships work. Here is the rub: "If I ask a volunteer to talk with Jane Smith, he will go out and ask Jane to be involved. Jane says, 'I will be delighted' and will pledge $100,000." In reality, Jane would have given a million if she had been properly cultivated by staff. Volunteers are critically important. Their biggest role in fundraising is to open the door."

Oxford, one of a handful of the world's top institutions, is very attractive to the men and women who say, "I am a son or daughter of Oxford." A visit by the president with a potential board member "is an honor, a place where serving the institution can be a wonderful partnership and it can be fun," he says.

At both Oxford and Toronto, the leaders of the campaigns were not the governing boards but campaign committees or cabinets. One such "son of Oxford" was invited to serve on the campaign cabinet. Jon says, "This leader and his family are not only thoughtful people, but very close to Oxford. Their foundation made the largest gift the university has received or his foundation has made." Their gift of £25 million will fund the development of the New Bodleian Library.

A great example of leadership, indeed.

Jon is also passionate about his staff's personal value system of commitment and continuity. Many development professionals jump from job to job, "probably for more money or a bigger title." To move an institution forward, we need excellent, committed staff over a longer period of time.

"I have learned so much about the engagement of volunteers over the years. One classic example was a time in my 40s when the president and I sat at lunch with a volunteer and asked him to consider a gift and he said 'no.'" Jon went on to say, "We at the University of Toronto don't understand no. We understand not right now or not for this cause. So let's keep talking."

A year later, when they celebrated the 100th gift of $100,000, this volunteer was that giver. "Sometimes it just takes knowing where they are and sticking with them."

This stellar professional has raised more money than any other professional in the business. If you ever have an opportunity to work with Dr. Jon Dellandrea, jump at it. I know I would.

Young P. Dawkins, III, Vice Principal for Advancement, University of Edinburgh

Currently the vice principal for development at the University of Edinburgh in Scotland, Young has also led ambitious programs as the president of the University of New Hampshire Foundation, Inc. (raising $102.8 million in less than three years) and earlier positions at Oberlin and Dartmouth Colleges. He is a past chairman of the board of trustees at Cheshire Academy. At every step of his professional life, he has broken all records in fundraising. He is well on his way to doing the same in Edinburgh.

"My job is to broker the relationships between the CEO and the board. These relationships are based on privileged information that must be handled delicately." When he and the principal are choosing members of the campaign board, for instance, nominees are often presented by a staff member who suggests they may be good for the board. Next, Young makes a personal visit with them, followed by a visit from the board chair. Finally, if the leader is thought to be the right person for the university, a meeting is set with the CEO. During all of these meetings, each representative looks for something that motivates the volunteers—they look for their passion. "At a university of the complexity of Edinburgh, the matching of the passions is easy to do," he stresses.

Before formally being invited to the campaign board, Young spends a great deal of time clearly articulating the role of the board because, he says, "This is a high-stakes game." From the university's point of view, they are looking for a leader who will bring support, advocacy, access, and wisdom. "That is happening right now," he explained. "Our Business School is preparing to take a major step forward on the most significant undertaking in its history. The school has a new dean. Because I am an information broker, I have put the dean together with a board member who is filled with both inspiration and vision, not to mention business acumen and wealth. The result will be a dean who learns from the board member how to inspire people to help him achieve his vision. The board member will become all the more engaged. He truly will have made a difference. Both will succeed because they understand that the institution is bigger than everyone else. Both will have changed the school for the better for all times."

When he was at the University of New Hampshire, they worked hard to build the board bond. Every board meeting was half work and half social. Three times a year the board was taken to interesting places: wine tours, horseback riding tours, and more. "When the board is bonded, they will band together to make something successful, as they did in the very short, highly successful campaign that gave 43 percent of the $103 million raised."

Young says, "I am in touch with all of my board all the time, at least once a month, and with some much more. It really is important to talk about small things, little things that are happening on campus."

There was a smile in his voice when he told this story: "There is a major arts festival taking place right now in Edinburgh. There is a tradition involving an upside-down purple cow during the festival. In my communication with the board this week, I mentioned that the cow was back up. They love this, and it encourages open, friendly e-mails in response."

Also, at every board meeting with this group, the last 45 minutes of the meeting includes a presentation led by an academic discussing his or her program. This can include students, tours, research, and more. "It is education, not training. The training is done one-on-one in the early days before one is asked to join the board."

"It would be naive to think that members of a board of a nonprofit would not be expected to make gifts, even stretch gifts, during their service. In the beginning, we do not specify the amount because we want their involvement to lead to greater giving. This is just like a venture capitalist who must have the lead financing to make the deal work. It is up to the staff to be confident in the product and the result the gifts will have in getting to fund that product," he says. "The best board members bring us their wisdom and involvement. We promise never to waste their passion or their time."

His advice to development professionals? "Be confident. Stroke the egos of the donors and board members, but get to the point."

No wonder Young Dawkins is the wunderkind of professional development leaders. Brave, bold, kind, and confident. Makes me want to take up the bagpipes!

Charles Phlegar, Vice President, Alumni Affairs and Development, Cornell University

Charlie is the vice president, alumni affairs and development at Cornell University, where he is the staff captain of Far Above: The Campaign for Cornell, which at this writing has achieved $2.2 billion on a $4 billion goal. Before taking the helm at Cornell, he was the interim vice president at Johns Hopkins, having moved up from senior associate vice president for development and alumni relations, where he was intimately involved in the more than $2 billion capital campaign. Earlier, he was vice president for development at the University of South Carolina, where he spearheaded the largest campaign in the university's history. Charlie has earned the credentials that place him in a very select group of high achievers. I think you will learn much from his words. Just listen.

Charlie has a warm feeling toward volunteers, and it shows. That warmth is balanced like a laser beam, however, by his commitment to metrics and accountability. Charlie says that "boards are critical for pure philanthropic investment, their networks, and for the strategic view they lend to university development."

"We, as staff, must embrace their business model to be successful. Boards understand that the strategic approach is critical to sustain passion and facilitate understanding. They are the knowledge carriers of historical events, and we rely on them to pass those on to their fellow alumni and to us as staff. They are the motivators and the encouragers for me and are critically important to helping me get what I need from the president and the deans."

Charlie admits that everyone knows they must bring dollars, but what they sometimes forget is that they are also needed as advocates for him with the individual colleges within the university. "Academics know they need dollars to function. It is easy to say 'I need,' but the volunteers understand how hard it is to make that happen."

"Boards are great advocates of progress," he says. "The executive committee wants to know I understand their needs, have a plan, a logistical path to success, and that I will be accountable. They want me to embrace that accountability."

Each board expects the same things: clear annual goals, a clear plan of how to get there, and a quarterly report on progress. The members of committees function as an executive committee to their area of interest, giving feedback on monthly reports and so on. They are the eyes and ears, supplying advice and confidence to Charlie as the CEO.

"I don't want more than advice and partnership. I ask selected board members to take on solicitations only because Cornell is known for active volunteer groups and participation. There is an active culture of participation by volunteers here. We ask boards to help us cultivate, address larger groups, host dinners, and attend alumni dinners and gatherings. Cornell's board has a public mission as a land grant college. This is the only top 10 university that has a portion of its colleges that are land grant colleges," he says. Therefore, Cornell's board is both self-selecting and publically appointed. The governor has political appointees because Cornell has four state-supported schools within the private university. Because of the public appointments, all board members in land grant colleges and public universities and organizations are not self-selected so not all are positioned to influence fundraising in a significant way.

"Our board members mix quite well. We provide a lot of social opportunities, and they all have a strong passion for higher education. There is a mix of wealth and business acumen on all boards here. When I was at Hopkins, there was a social aspect with personal friends that is so strong they have a hard time coming out of receptions to go to dinners," Charlie added.

"I am dealing with elite institutions that have big aha moments and, most often, a business mind-set that focuses on use of data and clear expectations of significant return on investments made in program growth. The data focus also helps trustees who may have an emotional attachment to a specific program overcome that bias and focus more on the strategic best interest of the university."

Charlie comments that many times staff members so want to please boards and donors that they will say "yes" to anything volunteers want. He urges staff to be prepared to defend with analytics why something should be different, why they cannot keep doing things the same way, and why they must tighten up their focus and their processes.

"Increasingly in our career, we want to relate to the board," Charlie argues. "We now have a university group looking at increasing our analysis work on all fronts. Can you imagine GE making their decisions by what a board member wants only? We need to put more investment into programs to look at data and mission balanced on program."

His board sees Charlie as a critical aspect of university business. "They want me to be professional, personable, aware of who they are, and appreciative of their gift of time. I respect them and they me, but they don't expect me to be their best friend. I try to keep a clear line of demarcation. I don't cross that line into friendship. I want to know them well, but I want to be careful not to cross the line of staff and board," he says.

In the future: Volunteers at Cornell give three times what nonvolunteers give. Volunteers have greater expectations of the organization if they give time. Much like all successful CEOs today, Charlie is putting more emphasis and attention on stewarding volunteers to assure that their experience—starting with their annual gift, which is usually self-identifying—is an excellent one. "We steward people in prospect layers, of course, by personal contacts, personal letters, and mostly reporting back on their efforts and their gifts to Cornell. Reports are personal, and those who fund endowments receive results of their dollars that are coming back to Cornell."

Charlie advises CEOs to think of stewardship as a part of the work that each assigned staff member owns. He prefers that one-to-one model to centralized stewardship because it requires staff to be more focused on the prospects they have beyond the gift, thus helping to keep important donors from falling through the cracks. This requires staff's welcoming advice from volunteers. The challenge is, he says, that staff members have to make decisions, while volunteers have a tendency to see the big picture. Because most often the volunteers are very bright and are often better at analysis than staff are, their suggestions are often powerful. While the staff is thinking, "I've just got to get this done," they are better off listening carefully to volunteers who are thinking, "How can I get this done better?"

"We have 400 staff. How do they all get an A-plus? The only way to make these relationships work is for staff to have clear directions."

Charlie concludes our discussion by saying, "I love getting input from volunteers. I am willing to listen to alumni about how to communicate and what to communicate. With technology, you can get specific and creative. We have learned that we cannot take every person and make him a donor. We now have clear expectations. Annual fund donors are self-selecting, and with good information we can be more focused on relationships and potential gift strategies toward major gifts. As staff members work with the boards, we must continue to be clearer in our communications and put processes in place to recruit and retain excellent board members. Too often, we do it off the cuff. We don't spell out what we want. We tell the board we expect an annual gift. We believe we must earn major gift."

Quite simply, says Charlie, "We must be more professional than ever."

Nigel Redden, Director, Spoleto Festival USA

Nigel Redden was named general director of Spoleto Festival USA in 1995. A graduate of Yale, he is responsible for all aspects of the festival, including fundraising, financial administration, marketing, union negotiations, artists' contracts, board development, and programming. He also leads the Lincoln Center Festival as director, and previously served as executive director of the Santa Fe Opera. He was born in Cyprus, his mother was from New Zealand, and he grew up in Italy—a great background to deal with the international nature of the Spoleto Festival that was co-founded with a sister festival in Italy. After going through very tough times with board and staff relations in the late 1980s, the festival, under Redden's leadership, has been thriving artistically and financially since his return in 1995.

Nigel alludes to the fact that the difficulty of changing board chairs requires the executive to adjust relationships frequently. "I have had many great chairs. Some are very busy executives who love the idea of the festival, know the personality of the region and the leadership, and clearly understand the pitfalls of missteps. The best of these leaders was one who always called me back within an hour, listened to my questions, and gave me an answer in 30 seconds. Another was a more national business leader who had a wide range of contacts, had been through tough business times, and knew how to roll with the punches. During his leadership, we could have gone down had he not put his credibility on the line for the festival. He turned us around financially. Another chaired during crisis times of change of staff leadership, but he was steadfast and took immense abuse unnecessarily. He had a real generosity of spirit."

Nigel stresses that he works to understand first what the board chair wants. Some want to be involved with the program, others become very engaged with a highly sophisticated analysis of numbers. Some simply want appropriate perks for events. Of course, the harder question is, "How can we get those we want most engaged? Clearly, there are people whose value to an organization is extremely high."

Nigel and his staff work hard to earn board member loyalty. Frankly, I loved hearing the word *earn.* It is such an appropriate word, but we rarely hear that from staff in this day of high expectations of board members. "It is hard, with a 60-member board, to have ongoing relationships. I find it best to stay in touch with each individual. Each is self-selecting with the depth of that relationship, however. Some want to stay in touch frequently, some are more spontaneous, and with some he struggles. Some don't want to be in touch other than at formally scheduled meetings and events."

"Europe is very different. With Americans, you have to earn the gift and it is hard work. With Europeans, the program is the focus because of significant governmental support for the arts." So with an international board, he has to understand cultural differences as well.

The engagement of the board is often best during the festival. "On some level, our board is our audience at large. Boards are our most involved audience members. They give the most articulate feedback. General audience members will vote with their feet. Clearly, boards have more direct response than the broad audience." Nigel also assesses how well he is doing by what board members give.

Clearly, the Spoleto board is a desirable seat for arts lovers. Asked how board members are chosen, he answers, "Very carefully."

Spoleto board meetings have become more open. Recently, the board engaged in deeply generative thinking. Led by one former management consultant years ago, a long-range plan was developed. Today, that plan has been completed and the festival is a success. The headquarters for the festival was in a historic building that was collapsing. The land on which the building sat was donated. If the board had not agreed to renovate the building, the festival would have been priced out of the rapidly increasing real estate market. A capital campaign was launched and was successful. Today, the headquarters is a pleasure for visitors as well as for staff. This project, too, took great skill in working with board members. One had the skills to oversee the renovation. While there was the inevitable "prickling" between a construction manager and the resident manager, the finished product was a prize for all.

Today, more generative thinking! Again because the real estate market in the urban area is in great demand, venues for performances were disappearing. The board has launched the fundraising to renovate numerous city-owned venues that will be used for Spoleto performances but so much more. What? Renovate a theater that is home to a local stage company? Yes. "Was it outside the festival's mission? Probably. But it was also the right thing to do and we had the capacity to do it."

What does Nigel advise other CEOs to think about as they strive to have a highly satisfied board? "Do a fair amount of checking on issues as they come up. Assess how close or far apart you are with your board member. While you may not always agree, at some point the chair of the board has to be the chair. At that point, you must accept with sincerity that they are wise and have the experience and wisdom to see what you may not be able to see at the moment."

No wonder so many board members seek to serve on this world-class board. What a world-class executive Nigel Redden is.

Conclusion

By the most modest standards, boards are asked to fulfill their minimum role: fiscal oversight, CEO hire and fire, and major strategic policies and decisions. The outcome of this book, I hope, is for CEOs and board members to understand how to create the rare board that really offers true, informed, constant value to the organizations they serve. We have learned that it is simple, really. It is about building a brain trust and allowing those brains to exercise, to engage.

What is it we want? This question plagues everyone from the development officer just out of college to the most seasoned executive of any organization. Based on the scores of interviews I conducted for this book, I believe that board members and CEOs, in the end, really want the same thing. In fact, we all do.

What all of us want most is for things to work. Plain and simple. Board members and CEOs, like the rest of us, want things to go well. They want people to be happy. They want to be productive. They want to get along. And, yes, they both want the world to be a better place. This includes having enough money to make a real difference.

I can easily spot happy and unhappy board members, those who are engaged and those who are not. Observing them led me to write this book.

I sought to uncover the truth about what it takes to make the board experience so very satisfying that it tickles members from head to toe. Or, on the flip side, what it is that makes some boards so numbing and unbearable that you don't want to return. I wanted to find out why some nonprofits are so successful, attract great leaders, and make a huge difference for the people they are organized to serve. But what I learned was so much more.

The truth of my discovery lies in relationships, the kind of relationships in which little things count as much as the big picture, and in which teamwork and collaboration can make a powerful impact. My partners in this effort told the truth. They told me about their experiences—the good, the bad, and everything in between. The common thread among them all is simple: They just want their ideas to be heard and their actions to have an impact on the organizations they serve.

We have told a story of board experiences across institutions and disciplines, geographic areas, and professional expertise, to weave a tapestry of those who drive our nonprofits. The main character throughout has been the "high-value board member," one who is wise and accomplished, one who has a fine reputation and excellent contacts, and one who is willing to give valuable time and assets to the organization. Such a person ends up being highly valued by the organization. By the time a person is highly valued, it is most likely that he or she has been exposed to a number of nonprofit experiences, good and bad. And we all must realize that those experiences have shaped their beliefs, their attitudes, and their expectations.

If we are to expect a board member to launch full bore into an organization and give all that he or she can in every way, the CEO must assure that member that the goals and the needs of the board members, the administrative leaders, and, yes, the staff of the organization and those they serve are well aligned.

Board members know when that alignment is present—they know because they not only feel good about their involvement but also are excited and passionate about the work of the organization and about its direction. For some, things just feel right when alignment has been achieved. For others, regular assessment and reflection tells them that what they want from their organization is what they are actually receiving.

Our leaders would agree that, absolutely, there must be:

- A written criteria for board membership and a job description for an A-plus board.
- Board members who are painstakingly chosen for their wisdom and passion for the mission, not necessarily to fill a particular skill set.
- A board composed of a diversity of opinions and backgrounds as long as all members can make a solid impact on board work.
- Active individuals who use their networks and contacts to stimulate funding security and awareness.
- Defined measurement of performance against their personal satisfaction of engagement.
- The means to support the organization financially.

For CEOs, however, that alignment can be more elusive.

How can a CEO measure, in a methodical way, the degree of alignment between board, leadership, and staff? How does he know when it is just right or out of kilter? How do we structure and monitor the best alignment? These questions led me to search for another final—and critical—truth and to develop the Board AlignMint™ model. This unique model outlines how to determine the best people fit and to build the trusting and enduring relationships among the board, the staff, and the organization.

AlignMint™ focuses on people and passion. It considers the kind of people board members want to be and those they want to be around. It considers what they want their fellow board members and senior staff to be like. And it takes into account the importance of passion for a mission a board member can believe in.

Those two elements—the people and the passion—combine to help drive the most important element of success: the progress of the organization. Progress is really the ultimate goal. Whether by way of more people impacted, a better community developed, or important improvements made to quality of life, when the most capable people are motivated by a genuine passion for the mission, they will act to secure philanthropic support, and progress will be the rewarding result.

Before an organization can implement the AlignMint™ model, it must first look carefully at both current and prospective board members as people. Would potential board members fit well with the existing leadership? Will they add value to the organization and the people? Will others like them? Admire them? Do the CEO's and the board members' skills and personalities complement each other?

Consider for a moment that in every organizational chart you will see the board clearly positioned over the staff. However, my research revealed that it doesn't work that way in effective organizations. While the staff does in fact report to the board, the best-aligned organizations really look more and act more interconnected than connected by straight lines usually seen in organizational charts.

In effective and successful organizations, the board and the CEO forge an interconnected partnership, shared, if you will. The board acts as a deliberative decision-making body that aids the CEO. They fashion the broad strategic plan and respond to the most challenging obstacles. In return, the CEO provides skilled executive leadership. He or she helps guide the board's deliberations. And, together, board members and the CEO alike are active participants who help the organization fulfill its mission.

The AlignMint™ model consists of three stages: Discovery, Building the Relationship, and Full Commitment. An organization undergoing an AlignMint™ assessment will move through these stages, gaining insight into both board and leadership motivators, strengths, and challenges and, ultimately, determine how aligned the wants and needs of both parties actually are.

A more comprehensive description of the AlignMint™ model and a complete questionnaire are available at www.corporatedevelopmint.com, but an abbreviated sample self-assessment follows here.

Appendix: AlignMint™

A SELF-ASSESSMENT TOOL FOR BOARDS AND LEADERSHIP

So now we know what makes board members tick, what makes them embrace a cause and give because it feels good in every way. It *is* the little things that count. We also know from our experiences and scores of studies that organizational alignment is one consistent measure of a well-oiled machine.

Alignment is the positioning of the board, staff, organization, community, and service recipients in the correct position to each other. Aligned, they each contribute something of great value. When the wheels on our cars are out of alignment, we can immediately feel a little shake. When we do not correct that, over time the car becomes almost impossible to drive. So too with organizations and institutions. For a smooth ride, we are looking for all components to be in alignment.

We focus here on the alignment of the board with its organization as a critical component of what is actually a complete system. That system—the board, the CEO, and the staff—must all be aligned in a way that allows them to support each other's efforts. Each piece of the system helps energize the whole.

How do you know when the organization, like the wheels on your car, begins to shake? When the people or systems are out of alignment? You diagnose the problem, right?

With wheels, it is simple. With organizations and institutions, diagnostics are quite a bit more complex. Generally, board members or the CEO simply know that things are working well or that they are not—that the wheels are shaking or not. The organization is simply just not "falling into place."

That is why we have developed the AlignMint™ Assessment. This in-depth assessment allows organizations to gain a clearer understanding of the root causes of the organization's underperformance. It allows the board, the CEO, and the staff to see more clearly what is not in alignment.

This Appendix will help you get started. I have provided a list of questions that will give a taste of how the full assessment would unfold. These questions will help you better understand what feelings, thoughts, and behaviors you should examine as a leader of an organization whose alignment is skewed. This tool will also help your board tell you what feels good to them and what is out of kilter. You want your board to work, lead, give, and ask others to do the same. You want them to bring their passion and wisdom to you. For this to happen, you must work in a way that gives them the best possible experience. To have each of you experience the joy of a fully aligned organization.

The questions should also give you a better sense of what a full AlignMint Assessment is like. And, depending on your answers to these questions, you may learn if an Assessment would benefit your organization.

Stage 1: Discovery

When the CEO/Board begins the process of finding a new addition to the board, and as a prospect considers joining a board, there are many important questions to consider. If you answer "no" to any of these questions, you are likely not digging deeply enough into the recruitment process.

Discovery: The CEO's Checklist

1. Think about the skills and talents this person has. Would those genuinely help us advance the work and the mission of this organization? And do we have the ability to use those skills well?
2. Is this a person with whom I could form a productive working relationship? Do we "click" effectively?
3. Is this person someone whose advice and guidance I would value?
4. Does this person feel a real sense of passion for our mission? If not, does he or she demonstrate a level of growing interest during the interviews that makes it clear that a passion can develop?
5. Does this person want to serve? (Some individuals may be tempted to say yes to serving, but may be acting more from a sense of obligation than real desire.)
6. Will this person constructively question the value of our actions and not serve as a rubber stamp?
7. Will this person debate the board and me on critical issues but once a decision is made exhibit loyalty and unanimity?
8. Will this person be a capable representative of one of the many diverse constituencies our organization serves?

Discovery: Board Prospect Checklist

1. Do I think I would learn from my fellow board members? Would I enjoy spending social time with them?
2. Do I admire my fellow board members?
3. Are there people on the board I want to know?
4. Do I believe the CEO is building his resume or is truly passionate for the cause?
5. Can I find a passion for this cause? If not passion, do I believe that this organization's mission is something

really important? During my discussions about joining the board, do I find myself becoming much more interested in the organization's work?

6. Are my talents and skills a good match for what this board needs? In other words, could I make a real difference here?
7. What would I want to do with/for this organization?
8. Will the CEO and board really value my opinions—no matter how revolutionary—and consider them with full objectivity?
9. Will I actually be able to influence this organization's future?
10. Is this an organization to which I would want to make a significant financial gift?

Stage 2: Building the Relationship

Obviously, the selection of good board members is only the first step in the AlignMint process. Effective working relationships must be developed over time and with effort.

That means that the next set of tasks will focus on developing productive working relationships. There are two key elements to that effort: the establishment of mutual trust and respect and the recognition that good relationships thrive on attention.

If you answer "no" to any of the following questions, trust has not been established between the CEO and the board, and your relationship is not getting the attention it needs to truly thrive.

For the CEO: Building the Partnership

1. Have I really uncovered what each board member wants from his or her involvement?
2. Do my board members trust and admire me? If not yet, what will I need to do to establish trust and earn respect?

3. Am I willing to earnestly consider and, if appropriate, follow this board's guidance?
4. Am I genuinely comfortable talking with board members before and after meetings? Are informal conversations with board members common?
5. Could I explain how each individual board member contributes something valuable to the board's work?
6. Do I really want more involvement from board members than simply writing a check?
7. Am I eager to attend board meetings, enjoy the debate, and admire its collective judgment?
8. Do I have a clear vision for the future of this organization?

For the Board Member: Building the Partnership

1. Do I look forward to attending the meetings?
2. Do I respect the work of the CEO?
3. Do I feel I am being valued as an individual?
4. Can I identify ways that my participation made a positive difference in the work of the board or the organization?
5. Are substantive matters discussed and acted upon while routine reporting is kept to a minimum?
6. Do they need my help?

Stage 3: Full Commitment

In the third stage, a well-aligned board and CEO will be firing on all cylinders. That is not to suggest that there will be no challenges, but with good alignment, board members and the CEO work productively to overcome obstacles by relying on a sense of partnership that allows all to contribute effectively.

Every "yes" answer below indicates that your CEO and board are fully aligned and you are both committed to the organization and its mission. If there are more "no" responses, one or both of you have not yet fully committed to the cause.

Constant, committed communication will bring you closer and closer into alignment.

For the CEO: Hallmarks of a Fully Aligned Board and CEO

1. On balance, do I look forward to board meetings?
2. Do I view the board more as a source of real help or as an organizational obligation?
3. At the end of board meetings, do I usually feel that meaningful work was accomplished?
4. Am I prepared to let the board make substantive decisions about the organization's future?
5. Have I grown in any valuable ways as a result of working with this board?
6. Do I have the skills to prepare for dynamic meetings?
7. Have I found a way for each member to engage in a meaningful way?

For the Board Member: Hallmarks of a Fully Aligned Board and CEO

1. With the exception of brand new initiates, do I enjoy and really know my fellow board members?
2. Have my relationships extended beyond the contact required to complete the work of the board?
3. Will I support the board and the CEO on decisions made as long as I am heard, and in the event I can't, will I speak up or duly resign from the board?
4. Am I content to focus on policy and leave day-to-day management to the CEO and staff?
5. Does the CEO share ideas and observations with me?
6. Do I want to make significant charitable investments to advance the mission of this organization?

Building an AlignMint board-CEO partnership takes work. The process outlined here will help you understand how much you and your organization have to do. If these short assessments make clear that you have some real work ahead, I would encourage you to visit Corporate DevelopMint's Web site (www.corporatedevelopmint.com) to learn more about AlignMint-guided approaches to board development. You will be glad you did.

About the Author

June Bradham

June Bradham is founder, owner, and president of Corporate DevelopMint, a fundraising and strategic planning consulting firm with more than twenty years of service to the nonprofit world. Without question, the firm's growth has been partly propelled by June's belief that nonprofit organizations play an absolutely central role in moving our communities and our society forward. In her eyes, the high-impact future of nonprofits must be guided by truly innovative leadership, clearly articulated visions, and an understanding that nonprofit success is invariably built on an ever-expanding network of positive relationships. The firm June founded two decades ago has grown from a one-person operation to a major presence in fundraising consulting. It is June's personal commitment to constant innovation and uncompromised quality that has led Corporate DevelopMint forward, year after year.

Having personally led and overseen a team that has led scores of fundraising campaigns with goals that have ranged from $2 million to over $1 billion, June has become a recognized leader in the development of innovative, successful development efforts. She was also honored by the *Charleston Regional Business Journal* as one of 2008's Most Influential Women in Business as the CEO of the Year, a testament to the strength of her for-profit acumen as well as her successes leading nonprofits.

June has also had the honor of contributing to the development community through published works and dozens of speaking engagements each year. She writes a monthly philanthropy column for the *Charleston Regional Business Journal* and has had a number of articles selected for magazine publications. June's expertise and insights have been shared with attendees at organizations as far ranging as the Association for Healthcare Philanthropy, the Council for the Advancement and Support of Education, the American Marketing Association, the Association for Fundraising Professionals International Conference and chapter events, the Association to Advance Collegiate Schools of Business, North and South Carolina Chambers of Commerce Executives, hospital associations, and Blackbaud's International Conference on Philanthropy. She is also proud to have been the very first alumna asked to present the convocation address to the graduating seniors of Columbia College.

June's deep commitment to the growth and success of nonprofit organizations is underscored by her years of volunteer experience, including current service as vice chair of the Columbia College Board, the executive committee of the Citadel Business School Board, the Moore School of Business at the University of South Carolina, and as a member of the AFP International Board, as well as the South Carolina Governor's School for Science and Math and Porter Gaud School Boards. She is a past president of the South Carolina Association of Nonprofit Organizations (SCANPO) and formerly served on the executive committees of the South Carolina State Chamber of Commerce Board, Association of Fundraising Professionals (AFP) Lowcountry Chapter, Spoleto Festival USA, and the Coastal Community Foundation of South Carolina Boards. June was recently named the Most Outstanding Woman of Distinction in the Economic Autonomy Category.

June holds a bachelor's degree from Columbia College. A Certified Fundraising Executive (CFRE), she completed the Harvard University Governance Education program in Cambridge, Massachusetts.

Corporate DevelopMint

Founded in 1987, Corporate DevelopMint has a deep history of transforming nonprofits into mission-driven organizations that thrive in even the most challenging philanthropic marketplaces. Hundreds of nonprofit organizations turn to Corporate DevelopMint, trusting in the depth of their experience and in their ability to craft fundraising programs built on relationships between organizations and donors. From strategic planning and foundation development to capital campaigns and planned giving programs, Corporate DevelopMint offers the expertise to customize programs that meet goals and help define a sound, sustainable plan for the future.

The Corporate DevelopMint team provides efficient service to clients throughout the United States. The firm also holds memberships in AFP, AHP, and the Council for Advancement and Support of Education (CASE). Consultant team members actively serve on the boards of nonprofit organizations and are invited to share their expertise at dozens of conferences and professional development events every year.

One of the main factors that differentiates Corporate DevelopMint from other fundraising consulting firms is the depth and breadth of its consultants' experience. These senior-level consultants come from the development offices of major universities and from the senior administration teams of large hospitals. They have led community-based human services organizations from community foundations to large-scale environmental organizations. They all have developed expertise in one or more fundraising tools, including planned giving, branding, and annual fund management, and they all have managed oversubscribed capital campaigns.

In addition to the human capital that makes Corporate DevelopMint a leader in the industry, it has designed and trademarked a number of proprietary tools to help nonprofits assess their current programs and capitalize on opportunities that those assessments highlight. Training modules, studies, and best practices research combine to offer Corporate DevelopMint clients an integrated suite of products designed to build and sustain long-term relationships, the cornerstone of every successful development program.

To learn about the firm, visit www.corporatedevelopmint.com.

Index